The serpent of Eden: a philological and critical essay on the text of Genesis III.

The serpent of Eden: a philological and critical essay on the text of Genesis III.

ISBN/EAN: 9783743304406

Manufactured in Europe, USA, Canada, Australia, Japa

Cover: Foto ©ninafisch / pixelio.de

Manufactured and distributed by brebook publishing software (www.brebook.com)

The serpent of Eden: a philological and critical essay on the text of Genesis III.

THE SERPENT OF EDEN.

THE SERPENT OF EDEN:

A PHILOLOGICAL AND CRITICAL ESSAY

ON THE

TEXT OF GENESIS III.,

AND

ITS VARIOUS INTERPRETATIONS.

BY

J. P. VAL D'EREMAO, D.D.,

MEMBER OF THE ANJUMUN-I-PUNJAB;
LATE RECTOR OF THE HOLY GHOST CHURCH, BASINGSTOKE,
NOW OF ST. MARY'S, DERBY,
AND CHANCELLOR OF THE DIOCESE OF NOTTINGHAM.

LONDON:
KEGAN PAUL, TRENCH & CO., 1, PATERNOSTER SQUARE.
1888.

(The rights of translation and of reproduction are reserved.)

TO
THE REV. SIR W. H. COPE, BART.

—•◦•—

DEAR SIR WILLIAM,

To no one can I more fitly dedicate this little book than to you, who have so kindly allowed me free access to your magnificent library at Bramshill Park, and have aided me with many a valuable suggestion. Without, therefore, making you responsible for any view here put forth, I offer it to you as a token of our mutual friendship, and in grateful acknowledgment of much kindness from you.

Believe me always, yours very faithfully,

JOSÉ P. VAL D'EREMAO.

BASINGSTOKE,
March 25, 1887.

PREFACE.

COMMENTATORS have always found great difficulty in interpreting Gen. iii.; and the difficulty has not diminished with time. A long-felt need exists of an interpretation satisfactory to science and human reason.

Such an interpretation I now beg to offer for the consideration of all classes of Christians, for here at least the interests of all shades of belief are identical. My sole object is to defend the truth of Holy Scripture against objections from science and reason.

It is neither my object nor my wish to prove that the received interpretations, given in the past, are either false or absolutely untenable. Where I have used such words as "untenable" I wish to be understood, not as absolutely condemning the theory or interpretation to which I apply it, or as declaring it to be utterly incorrect. I mean to say only that the difficulties and objections raised against it are, to my mind and from my point of view, so strong and cogent as to render that theory or interpretation utterly untenable to my reason. Those difficulties, during years of reading and reflection, have always kept increasing to my mind ; and the explanations given to obviate or meet those difficulties have continually become less and less satisfactory. Many others, doubtless, have felt and feel as I do.

I have tried to state these difficulties fairly and fully, yet moderately. The chief among them, from my point of view, is common to every past interpretation. It is that they all deal largely in gratuitous suppositions, which are absolutely without any foundation in the letter of the sacred narrative, as given in Gen. iii.

Those who find no difficulty in that narrative, and those whose minds are satisfied with any of the interpretations hitherto given, are welcome to hold such interpretations, and to defend them to the best of their ability. Those, however, who have felt the force of the many and serious difficulties attending Gen. iii. are invited to consider the interpretation now offered.

J. P. VAL D'EREMAO.

BASINGSTOKE,
Feast of St. Hilary,
January 14, 1887.

CONTENTS.

CHAPTER		PAGE
I.	OBJECT STATED	1
II.	THE SACRED NARRATIVE	5
III.	VARIOUS THEORIES ON THE MANNER OF THE TEMPTATION BY "THE SERPENT"	15
IV.	DIFFICULTIES ATTENDING TEMPTATION BY A BESTIAL SERPENT	32
	SECT. I., AS ACTING OF ITSELF	32
	SECT. II., AS POSSESSED BY SATAN	66
V.	OBJECTIONS AGAINST PROPOSING A NEW THEORY	72
VI.	THE NEW THEORY	77
VII.	THE CURSE ON "THE SERPENT"	97
VIII.	ORIGIN OF THE COMMONLY RECEIVED INTERPRETATION	117
IX.	CONNECTION BETWEEN GEN. III. AND SERPENT-WORSHIP	127
X.	WHAT IS THE WEIGHT OF THE ARGUMENT FROM SERPENT-WORSHIP?	130

CHAPTER		PAGE
XI.	WAS SERPENT-WORSHIP UNIVERSAL?	135
XII.	ORIGIN OF SERPENT-WORSHIP	151
XIII.	CONCLUSION	160

APPENDIX.—HEBREW AND GREEK TEXTS OF THE SACRED NARRATIVE 171

THE SERPENT OF EDEN.

CHAPTER I.

OBJECT STATED.

THE temptation of Eve by "the Serpent" has been, on all hands and always, viewed as a matter full of mystery. This mystery is by no means satisfactorily explained by the various interpretations given by commentators to its attendant circumstances, as given in the sacred narrative. It contains an acknowledged difficulty, and a great one.

To both Jews and Christians alike, the narrative of the temptation and fall of man is an article of faith. It is the very foundation of the edifice of faith; the very groundwork of the whole scheme of redemption. It is an article of faith that Eve was tempted by "the Serpent," and fell;—that she, in her turn, tempted Adam, who also fell;—and that Adam, Eve, and this "Serpent" were subjected each to a special condemnation by God, in punishment of the sin which each had committed. But who or what that "Serpent" was;—and in what way he tempted Eve;—and in what precisely his condemnation consisted;—and in what manner it worked in him :—these are details which have never been defined as articles of faith. Provided, therefore, that we do not violate the laws of scriptural interpretation, we are free to choose such explanations of these details as may suit our individual reason. The manner and means of the temptation have been and are still matters of discussion, in which, if the substantial and literal truth of the sacred narrative be held intact and inviolate, opinions on details may well be left free. *In necessariis unitas; in dubiis libertas.*

Now, while the faithful, holding fast to the facts of the temptation and fall, seek to explain their attendant circumstances as best they may, to unbelievers the whole narrative has long been a choice object of ridicule and a rich source of amusement. They assert that here, in the very beginning of the scriptural history of the human race, the narrative lays before us a mass of glaring absurdities and improbabilities. They declare that a bestial serpent could not possibly tempt Eve ;—that Eve would certainly have been surprised and startled and alarmed at hearing a dumb animal speak with a human voice ;—that it is no real curse for the serpent to go on its belly ;—that it is not a fact that it eats dust at all. Commentators have striven to reply to these and other important objections with more or less ability and learning. But we must candidly acknowledge that they have not been so successful as we could wish them to be, in so important an encounter. With every wish to believe and to accept any reasonable interpretation, even the faithful still find the difficulty unsolved, though they believe simply because God so teaches. But it is not at all likely that such explanations will satisfy those whose faith is anything but strong and deep.

Under these circumstances, and considering the many unsolved difficulties attending the commonly received opinion, I think that scarcely any apology is necessary for offering an interpretation which seems to give a very full and complete solution to all those difficulties. Before proceeding, however, to give this interpretation, it will add to the clear understanding of the whole question regarding the serpent of Gen. iii., if I first give the sacred narrative itself, with the various interpretations till now advanced to explain its details, and the objections that are made against it.

CHAPTER II.

THE SACRED NARRATIVE.

I HERE give the sacred narrative from the Authorized English Version, side by side with the rendering of the Douay Bible from the Latin Vulgate; and I place at the foot as literal a translation as I am able to make from the original Hebrew text.

Authorized Version.	*Douay Version.*
Gen. iii. 1. Now the serpent was more subtil than any beast of the field which the Lord God had made. And he said unto the woman, Yea, hath God said, Ye shall not eat of every tree of the garden?	Gen. iii. 1. Now the serpent was more subtle than any of the beasts of the earth which the Lord God had made. And he said to the woman, Why hath God commanded you that you should not eat of every tree of Paradise?
2. And the woman said unto the serpent, We may eat of the fruit of the trees of the garden:	2. And the woman answered him *saying:* Of the fruit of the trees that are in Paradise we do eat,
3. But of the fruit of the tree which *is* in the midst of the	3. But of the fruit of the tree which is in the midst of Para-

garden, God hath said, Ye shall not eat of it, neither shall ye touch it, lest ye die.

4. And the serpent said unto the woman, Ye shall not surely die.

5. For God doth know that in the day ye eat thereof, then your eyes shall be opened, and ye shall be as gods, knowing good and evil.

. . . . .

13. And the Lord God said unto the woman, What *is* this *that* thou hast done? And the woman said, The serpent beguiled me, and I did eat.

14. And the Lord God said unto the serpent, Because thou hast done this, cursed *art* thou above all cattle, and above every beast of the field; upon thy belly shalt thou go, and dust shalt thou eat all the days of thy life:

15. And I will put enmity between thee and the woman, and between thy seed and her seed; it shall bruise thy head, and thou shalt bruise his heel.

dise, God hath commanded that we should not eat, and that we should not touch it, lest perhaps we die.

4. And the serpent said to the woman, No; you shall not die the death.

5. For God doth know that in what day soever you shall eat thereof, your eyes shall be opened and you shall be as gods, knowing good and evil.

. . . . .

13. And the Lord God said to the woman, Why hast thou done this? And she answered, The serpent deceived me, and I did eat.

14. And the Lord God said to the serpent, Because thou hast done this, cursed art thou among all cattle and beasts of the earth; upon thy breast shalt thou go, and dust shalt thou eat, all the days of thy life.

15. And I will put enmities between thee and the woman, and thy seed and her seed, she shall crush thy head, and thou shalt lie in wait for her heel.

Hebrew.

Gen. iii. 1. And the serpent was intelligent among all living (beings) of the field which the Lord God had made. And he said to the woman: Strange! that God has said, Ye shall not eat of every tree of the garden!

2. And said the woman to the serpent, Of the fruit of (each) tree of the garden we may eat.

3. But of the fruit of the tree which (is) in the midst of the

garden, God hath said, Ye shall not eat of it and shall not touch it, lest perhaps ye die.

4. And said the serpent to the woman, Not dying shall ye die.

5. For God knoweth that in the day ye eat of it, your eyes will be opened, and ye shall be as gods, knowing good and evil.

. . . . . .

13. And said the Lord God to the woman, What (is) this thou hast done? And said the woman, The serpent deceived me, and I did eat.

14. And said the Lord God to the serpent, Because thou hast done this, cursed (*art*) thou above every beast and every living (being) of the field. Upon thy belly thou shalt go, and dust thou shalt eat, all the days of thy life.

15. And enmity I will put between thee and between the woman; and between thy seed and between her seed. He shall crush thy head, and thou shalt crush his heel.

Such is the sacred narrative, which forms the subject of our discussion. Well known as it is to us all from our earliest days, it will still repay a serious and detailed consideration.

It will be useful for us to note that the literal translation given above differs, in some important particulars, from the existing versions in the English language. Let us consider each point of variance.

1. In ver. 1, I have put the word "intelligent" instead of "subtil." The Hebrew word is עָרוּם (*gharûm*). This conveys the idea of something more than mere animal subtility or cunning. It is derived from the word עָרַם (*gharam*), which primarily means "he made naked," "he discovered."

Hence proceeds the secondary meaning of discovery by the intellect or reason—discursive speculation. In consequence of this, it is used in the Holy Scriptures to indicate the rational qualities of prudence or wisdom. In this sense we find the very word which is here used in Gen. iii. 1, applied repeatedly to the prudent or wise man, in contrast with the foolish. Thus, in Prov. xii. 16, " A fool's wrath is presently known ; but a *prudent* man covereth shame." And further on, in ver. 23, "A *prudent* man concealeth knowledge ; but the heart of fools proclaimeth foolishness." It is unnecessary to multiply instances of this exact meaning of this word.

So, too, the Greek Septuagint gives the word φρονιμώτατος, which is derived from φρονέω. To this root Schrivellius gives the meanings *intelligo, cogito, sentio, judico, delibero,*—" I understand," " I think," " I perceive," " I judge," " I deliberate." This is also the scriptural meaning of the word. In Matt. x. 16, where our Lord says, " Be ye therefore wise as serpents," the word used is the positive degree, of which the superlative is used in Gen. iii. 1: φρόνιμοι ὡς οἱ ὄφεις. Here too, then, in the Septuagint, as in the Hebrew, a word is used which distinctly shows us that the " Seventy interpreters" understood the Hebrew text to indicate the intention of the sacred writer as meaning that the Serpent was subtil, if you like, but with an intelligent, thinking, and reasoning subtility. Otherwise they would not have used the word φρονιμώτατος.

The Ancient Arabic Version, too, uses the word *hakmimunh*, which signifies "wisest."

In the Greek and the Arabic, the expression is in the superlative degree. In the Hebrew language, which has no superlative *form* for the adjective, the superlative *sense* is indicated by the words "above all," or "among all:" this is also done in the text, Gen. iii. 1.

Add to all this, that where the Latin Vulgate uses the word *callidior*—"more subtil,"—St. Augustine, in his "Genesis ad Literam" (*in loc.*), citing the Vetus Itala, or Old Italian Bible, says in one place, "serpens autem erat prudentissimus," and in another place, "erat sapientissimus omnium bestiarum quæ sunt super terram." "Most prudent," "most wise," surely indicate reasoning powers, and not mere animal cunning.

The Greek Septuagint, the Vetus Itala, and the Ancient Arabic all agree, therefore, with the original Hebrew text, in giving words which signify, not mere animal cunning, but something really rational and intelligent. We must conclude, therefore, that the subtility which the text predicates of this Serpent is an intelligent, thinking, and reasoning subtility. The importance of this conclusion we shall soon perceive.

2. In this same first verse, the word which our English versions render "beasts" has, in the Hebrew, a far more general sense. It is חַיָּה (*chaiath*), which means any *living being*, and not merely a beast. It is from the same root as "life." When God breathes the breath of life into Adam, and he becomes a *living* soul, the same word is used; and it is used also when (Gen. iii. 20) Eve is called *Chavvah*, because she is to be the mother of all living—meaning men. This is the plain scriptural use of the word, in confirmation of which numerous other examples could be adduced. It follows, therefore, from this usage, and from the original meaning of this word, that we are precluded from limiting the comparison of this Serpent's subtility to other *beasts* only. The comparison extends to *all living beings of the earth;* for the word "field" is plainly synonymous with "world."* Therefore it includes all beasts,

* "Field" is not used in its restricted sense, as is evident, because

and man himself; and possibly also some angels who minister on earth. God alone seems to be excluded from this comparison, as the Creator of all; for the comparison is urged in the fullest and widest sense, asserting that this "Serpent was the most intelligent among all living beings on the earth which the Lord God has made."

That this important extension of the comparison is correct, is confirmed by the wording of ver. 13 in this same chapter. Here the serpent is declared accursed "above all *beasts*" (בְּהֵמָה, *behemah*), and also "above all living beings" (חַיָּה, *chaiath*). "Cattle" and "beasts," as given in the English versions, is a mere meaningless tautology, which does not exist in the original Hebrew. There, two distinct words are used, the one applicable to beasts alone; the other, by its very derivation, including all "living beings." The text, therefore, indicates that this Serpent was the most intelligent among all living beings, even including man himself; which, as we shall see, is another important point.

3. In this same ver. 1 the Serpent's speech to

otherwise it would needlessly exclude the beasts or living beings of the mountains, of the air, and of the sea—that is a large proportion of animated nature; and it would thus weaken that very superiority in subtility which it is meant to emphasize.

Eve opens with the interjection, אַף־כִּי (*Aph-ki*). This word is not an interrogation, as rendered in the Vulgate "*Quare?*" and the Douay Version "Why?" Nor is it a mere exclamation, as in the Authorized Version, "Yea," with an interrogation after it. The Greek Septuagint approaches nearer the mark: Τί, ὅτι, "What! that God," etc. The precise meaning, however, of *Aph-ki* is an exclamation of surprise—"Strange! that," or, "It is a strange thing that." Slight as this difference may at first sight appear, it is not without importance in considering the manner of the temptation. If we put the temptation as a direct question (as it is in the English versions) it may lead the mind to imagine a visible and audible questioner. But the plain Hebrew interjection, "Strange! that God hath said, Ye shall not eat of every tree in the garden," sounds much more like an internal suggestion to the mind, put forth as if it proceeded from Eve's own thoughts.

4. In ver. 14 the word "belly" is very correctly translated from the Hebrew word גָּחוֹן (*ghechon*). Yet it is necessary, in order to understand the nature of the curse, to point out the derivation of this word; because by means of this derivation we shall see that this passage becomes more

intelligibly and naturally connected with other passages of Scripture, which will be adduced later on to explain the nature of the curse. *Ghechon*, then, is derived from the root גָּחַן (*ghachan*), which originally signifies "he bent," "he bowed down," "he was curved." In the word *ghechon*, therefore, we not only have the meaning of "belly," but, included in that meaning, we have the idea of bending or bowing down to the ground; because the "bellies" of almost all animals except man are turned earthwards; and even man, when bowing before a superior, necessarily bends his belly towards the ground. This will have to be recalled to mind when we are considering parallel passages of Scripture, with the view of ascertaining the precise meaning of the curse.

These four points will prove to have a very important bearing on the question, What or who is this Serpent? It is very necessary that we should keep them constantly in our minds, while we investigate the various theories regarding the temptation, and weigh the arguments used against the commonly received interpretation of Gen. iii.

I have not thought it expedient to discuss the question whether, in ver. 15, the correct rendering should be "he shall crush" or "she," "his heel" or "her." It does not concern our present subject; and, as it has been repeatedly discussed, those interested may find the subject treated in numerous works. Both renderings understand and admit that the agent in crushing the serpent's head is the seed of the woman, our Lord Jesus Christ.

CHAPTER III.

VARIOUS THEORIES ON THE MANNER OF THE TEMPTATION BY "THE SERPENT."

WE need not waste time on Rabbinical and Koranic theories of the manner in which the Serpent tempted Eve. They are not only palpably absurd in themselves, but they are also quite foreign to the purpose in hand. They aggravate rather than solve the difficulties that we have to consider. I proceed, therefore, to state the other principal theories which have been, at various times and by various writers, upheld, in explanation of the circumstances of the temptation by the Serpent.

I.

Some Jewish and Christian authors have contended that the whole narrative of the temptation and fall is an allegory, written by Moses in order to convey a deep spiritual meaning. But this cannot be.

If they found their deep meaning on the denial of the historical truth (as a fact) of this sacred narrative, then neither Jews nor Christians can admit such an explanation. We may and do admit that a deep spiritual meaning can be derived from this, as from other passages of Scripture; but still we must and do hold the facts there stated to be historical truths. The whole narrative speaks as of a fact. It so interlaces the acts and words of God, Adam, Eve, and the Serpent; of the creation, the temptation, and the fall; that if the truth of any one part is denied, varied, or changed into a mere allegory, then the whole falls to pieces, or can be held only as a mere allegory. It is a case of all or none.

But there is a further objection against this view. What, I ask, is an allegory? An allegory is a *spiritual* interpretation, given in addition to the admission of *natural* facts; and it therefore necessarily presupposes those natural facts. By an allegory, a second interpretation is built upon the natural and literal one, as the second story of a house is built upon the first. It is thus that St. Paul (Gal. iv. 21 and following verses) allegorizes on the history of Isaac and Ishmael. But he holds unquestioned, nay, he presupposes, in their full integrity, the historical facts narrated in Gen. xxi. In truth, without the previous admission of those facts, his allegory could have no existence, any more than a second story of an edifice can stand without the first. Such is the very nature of an allegory. When it is stated, therefore, that the narrative in Gen. ii. and iii. is an allegory, it must first of all be admitted that it is a true statement of historical facts. If not, then it must be asserted that the whole is a mere fable or myth. The latter no one, not even the authors of this theory, can admit. But if we once admit as an historical fact what is there narrated, then the difficulties, whatever they are, must still continue to exist as before, notwithstanding a mythical or allegorical explanation. The building up of an allegory upon those facts will not help to remove the difficulties attending the circumstances of those facts.

This theory may, therefore, be at once rejected; because it either denies the literal truth of the sacred narrative, and is therefore subversive of faith; or it admits the truth of that narrative, and then it leaves the difficulties absolutely unsolved as before.

II.

A metaphorical interpretation has been given by some, in the sense that by the story of the serpent and the forbidden fruit is meant the giving way by Adam and Eve to the pleasures of the flesh.

This silly absurdity is easily and briefly refuted by referring to Gen. i. 28. There the precept to "increase and multiply"—(and in the case of Adam and Eve, then the only human beings, it was not only a benediction, but also an actual command)—was given prior to the prohibition in Gen. ii. 17. The union of man and wife, therefore, was not only not the subject of that prohibition; on the contrary, it was expressly commanded. Hence they could not have sinned by obeying a direct command of God.

Moreover, the rules of correct interpretation forbid us to adopt a metaphorical sense in an historical narrative, such as is that of the temptation by the Serpent. It is also an express and acknowledged rule in scriptural interpretation, that the literal sense is not to be abandoned for a metaphorical one, without good and evident reason. Here there is no reason at all for a metaphorical explanation, except the difficulties attending the common interpretation. Those difficulties, however, do not furnish a sufficient reason for admitting a metaphorical sense, because (as we shall see hereafter) they can be overcome without abandoning the literal historical sense of the narrative. The narrative, therefore, cannot be taken in this metaphorical sense.

III.

Among the theories to be at once rejected is that the bestial serpent was, *himself and naturally*, the tempter. If this were ever seriously put forward by any sane man, the physical impossibility of an irrational animal, unaided by any higher power, being able to talk with a human voice and to reason, would be quite enough to refute it.

IV.

Some commentators, especially of the Protestant school, headed by Bishop Patrick, have elaborated a theory that the temptation of Eve was accomplished by the devil appearing to her as an angel from God, in a brilliant, flying, serpentine form, which they assert to be the form under which the seraphim are described in the Scriptures.

But the following considerations must make us unhesitatingly reject this theory :—

1. It is a purely gratuitous supposition; for in the scriptural narrative there is not a word to indicate that the tempter came in the form of an angel. There it is "the Serpent" who tempts; and no mention is made of any other tempter.

2. The seraphim are not represented in Scripture as having serpentine forms, as these authors assert. For in Isa. vi. 2 and following verses, the seraphim are said to "stand," to "cover their feet," and to hold a "coal of fire in his hand." They have, therefore, feet, legs, and hands, in addition to wings. In no sense, therefore, can they be said to have serpentine bodies or forms.

3. The word שָׂרָף (*seraph*, plural *seraphim*) does not, in Hebrew, mean a "serpent" or "serpentine body," as is erroneously stated by these authors. It is an adjective, and not a substantive noun. It simply signifies "fiery," "burning," or "ardent."

4. Even if in any other passage of the Scripture *seraph* were used to signify "a serpent," that would not help their argument in the case of Gen. iii. Here the word used is not *seraph* at all, but נָחָשׁ (*nachash*), which is derived from quite a different

root, and signifies "the hisser," indicating the peculiar sound made by the serpent.

It seems difficult at first sight to account for the origin of so erroneous a theory. But, on further investigation, it will be found to have arisen from a misunderstanding of Numb. xxi. 6 and following verses. There, the fiery serpents sent among the Israelites for their sins are called הַנְּחָשִׁים הַשְּׂרָאפִים (*hannechashim hasseraphim*); that is to say, "burning or fiery serpents." Further on Moses is ordered to make a brazen שָׂרָף (*saraph*), that is to say, a "brazen fiery one," *nachash* (serpent) being understood. This, in the English versions, as also in the Vulgate, has been translated "a brazen serpent," which gave rise, doubtless, to the erroneous idea that in Hebrew *seraph* meant a "serpent." Hence these commentators concluded that the angelic seraphim must be angels with serpentine forms; whereas in truth they are so called because in a special manner they are "burning, fiery, and ardent angels." On this light and unstable foundation was erected this pretentious but untenable theory.

Besides, the tempter nowhere represents himself as an angel.

Moreover, Eve might, to a certain extent, have

been excusable, if she had yielded to a supposed messenger from God.

The whole theory, therefore, is, from beginning to end, a groundless supposition in every detail, besides being opposed to the literal wording of the sacred narrative; it cannot, therefore, be admitted.

V.

A few commentators have not rested content with holding that the tempter assumed the form and status of an angel from God. They have gone the extravagant length of holding that he "assumed the form of the Son of God" in order to tempt Eve.

What they mean by "the form of the Son of God" I really cannot conceive. For the Divinity has no visible form; and a human form was not united to the Son of God till nearly four thousand years afterwards, in the Incarnation, of even the possibility of which Eve could then have had no idea. Whatever they may mean, it will be sufficient to point out, in refutation of this (as of the preceding) theory, that Eve's acting upon an apparent instruction from God Himself would not have been a sin at all. But, in addition to this, the very words of the sacred narrative give a flat contradition to this, as to the preceding theory. Reperuse the words of the tempter in Gen. iii. 4, 5. He not only does not so represent himself as either an angel from God or as the Son of God; but he clearly, distinctly, and openly manifests a direct opposition to God, against whose command he plainly and deliberately urges Eve. He also flatly contradicts the efficacy of God's threat of death.

The theory, moreover, is a purely gratuitous supposition, and clearly against the letter of Scripture.

It seems difficult to account for the proposition and adoption of such evidently erroneous and palpably incorrect views, by men of intellect and learning, except on the fact of the admitted difficulties experienced in interpreting Gen. iii. Like drowning men, they have grasped at straws.

VI.

Another theory is that the tempter was Satan, who assumed the visible but unsubstantial and apparitional form of a serpent—just as angels have appeared as men, and the Holy Ghost, at one time as a dove, and at another as "parted tongues as it were of fire"—and that Satan then caused the sound of a human voice to proceed from the jaws of this apparition, which Eve took to be a living, bestial serpent.

This theory also labours under the insurmountable objection, that it is a purely gratuitous assertion, without the shadow of a foundation in the words of the sacred narrative. There we have not even a hint of there having been an apparition, and not "the Serpent" in his natural *reality*. Besides, as Eve, in this supposition, must have taken it for a living, bestial serpent, all the difficulties which beset the next following and commonly received theory would, under this interpretation, still remain untouched. This theory, therefore, is as useless as it is opposed to the literal wording of Gen. iii.

VII.

The generally received theory is that the tempter (Satan) entered into the body of one of the bestial serpents then existing in Eden, and took possession of it, as he did, in after times, of the *energumeni*, or possessed persons, mentioned in the Gospels; that he used the vocal organs of this serpent for his purpose, forming a human voice in the serpent's mouth, and discoursing thence with Eve, as one might through a mask, or as the evil spirits used to reply to our Lord, according to the Gospels, out of the mouths of possessed persons. That Satan is endowed with, and has been allowed to exercise, similar powers, we know from the Scriptures themselves, not to mention the cases of the pagan oracles.

This theory has been so commonly propounded and accepted as the only one which holds steadfastly to the literal sense of the sacred narrative, that most readers will doubtless be surprised at my saying that it also is a purely gratuitous supposition, which has not the slightest foundation in the words of Gen. iii.! Where, I ask, is there one single word indicating to us the presence of any other being except "the Serpent," himself alone? Nowhere! Is there one single word anywhere to show us that the sacred writer meant that "the Serpent" was possessed, or was acting under the coercion of a higher being, or was not himself the one, free, deliberate, and actual agent? Not one word! All through it is, "the Serpent was,"—"the Serpent said,"—Eve, and afterwards God, "said to the Serpent;"—"the Serpent" always, and not any one who possessed it, or acted in or by it. No evil spirit is mentioned at all. There is not the remotest trace of the presence or action of any other being except "the Serpent." All that is said and done, is said and done to or by "the Serpent," and "the Serpent" alone. Whence, then, comes this theory of Satanic possession? Certainly not from the literal wording of the sacred narrative. That says nothing of Satanic possession; it clearly and distinctly and simply attributes the temptation to "the Serpent" alone. Satan's entering the serpent's body and possessing it, and speaking by means of it, are all gratuitous assumptions on the part of these commentators; and they are all directly contradictory of the literal sense of the text. My first objection, therefore, against this theory, as against others, is that it violates this literal sense of the sacred narrative, and is a mere hypothesis.

Besides this, Eve must have taken the serpent to be a mere bestial serpent, because she could not have known that it was possessed by any superior power. She had no previous knowledge of such an event or of its possibility. Hence to her mind it would have been only a bestial serpent, talking and reasoning in a manner in which she knew that bestial serpents could not talk and reason. Hence all the difficulties besetting temptation by an apparitional serpent would still continue to exist in the supposition of a Satanic possession of the serpent.

Nay, this would add a few more difficulties to those already besetting the narrative, as we shall see in the next chapter. For the present, it is quite enough to say that this theory does not lessen the difficulties of interpreting Gen. iii., and that it is a gratuitous supposition, opposed to the literal wording of the text.

To hold this theory we should be obliged to add to the words of the text, and to put constructions upon those words which they do not naturally bear. For instance, we should be obliged to say, "The serpent was (not, indeed, himself the most subtil, but, having been temporarily possessed by the superior power and intelligence of one of the rebel angels, he for a little while seemed to be) the most subtil of all the beasts of the field." What a long and self-contradictory parenthesis is this which we should have to insert, especially as, after all, it flatly contradicts the plain words, " The serpent *was* the most subtil"! Again, the words "He said to Eve" would have to be changed thus: "He (did not himself speak to Eve, but Satan who possessed him used his vocal organs and caused a human speech to issue from the serpent's jaws, by which, not the serpent, but Satan) said to Eve." And so on. Each clause which the sacred narrative clearly assigns to the Serpent alone would have to be explained away, as referring, *not* to the serpent, *but* to Satan who possessed him. Surely this is doing fearful and needless violence to the literal sense of the Scriptures! How differently the Scriptures speak of Satanic acts and words in the cases of real possession, we may easily see in the Gospels. There the acts and words are clearly and unmistakably referred to the evil spirits, though there was the less necessity for so doing, because it had already been stated that the men were possessed by the devil. Here, in Genesis iii., no such antecedent announcement is made; the words are not attributed to Satan, and no indication is given of his presence. The usage of Scripture, therefore, together with the absence of any hint of Satanic possession, convinces us that this theory is opposed to the literal and obvious sense of the sacred narrative.

I have put this argument at a greater length than absolute necessity required, because this theory has been most erroneously called the "only literal interpretation" of Gen. iii. To this it has not the remotest claim. The fact is precisely the reverse. Whatever other merit this theory may or may not have, it is most evidently and most certainly *not* a literal interpretation of this narrative. Yet under this false pretence it has succeeded only too long in usurping in Christian literature a most notable place, to which it is in no way entitled.

VIII.

One writer only, that I know—Cardinal Cajetan—seems to have put aside all idea of either a Satanic apparition, or of a Satanic possession, or of a myth; and to have propounded a novel idea. He holds that the temptation was a purely internal temptation; that it was not an audible or visible temptation; that it did not, therefore, need either an apparitional or a bestial serpent. In fact, he seems to dispense with "the Serpent" altogether. This, of course, raises against his theory the insurmountable objection that the Scripture most distinctly and positively teaches that "the Serpent" did tempt Eve. No theory which excludes "the Serpent" is consistent with the requirements of the sacred narrative.

IX.

Our interpretation, which (as will be seen hereafter) avoids all difficulty, is that "the Serpent" is —in Gen. iii. as elsewhere—only another scriptural name for Satan. Of this interpretation I shall here say no more, as it will be fully considered in Chapter VI.

Of the preceding eight theories, none seems to deserve any serious consideration except that given under No. VII., p. 24, which is the commonly received one. The question, therefore, may be narrowed to this one point.

The Scripture tells us plainly that "the Serpent" tempted Eve. This Serpent was either a bestial serpent, or it must have been some other serpent, not a bestial one, if such a one we can find mentioned in the Scriptures.

If it was the bestial serpent, as the commonly received theory maintains, then it must have acted either by its own natural powers or under a higher influence. That it could have tempted Eve of its own natural powers is a physical impossibility. That it did so under a higher influence is a mere gratuitous supposition, not only unsupported by the plain words of the sacred narrative, but positively contradicting them.

We are, therefore, left under the necessity of seeking out from the Scriptures themselves if there be not some "Serpent" other than a bestial one. But before we do so, let us suppose, for the time being, that the bestial serpent is the one here indicated, in order that we may realize how many and how great are the difficulties attending the commonly received theory.

CHAPTER IV.

DIFFICULTIES ATTENDING TEMPTATION BY A BESTIAL SERPENT.

THESE difficulties may be placed under two heads: (1) those which tell against the serpent considered as a mere bestial serpent; and (2) those which tell against the serpent as having acted under the coercion of a superior Satanic power.

SECTION I.—*Difficulties attending Temptation by a mere Bestial Serpent.*

I.

If "the Serpent" was a mere bestial serpent, how came he to become "more subtil" than other serpents in Eden? In the Hebrew text, we not only have the definite article before the word "Serpent," הנחש (*hannachash*), and in the Septuagint also ὁ ὄφις, "*the* Serpent;" but the Hebrew text also expressly inserts the substantive verb "was," הָיָה (*hayah*): הַנָּחָשׁ הָיָה (*Hannachash hayah*), "the Serpent was." The use of the definite article and of the substantive verb, according to the idiom of the Hebrew language, precludes the possibility of the proposition being a general one, asserted generically of all serpents, or of the whole serpent race. In such general propositions, in the Hebrew language, the substantive verb ("was" or "is") is always understood, and is never expressed. I need not cite the numerous instances which we find, in the Book of Proverbs for instance, to prove this fact. The text, therefore, cannot mean that all serpents, or the whole serpent race in general, were "more subtil than all the beasts of the field." It states that one particular, definite "Serpent was *the* most subtil of all living beings in the world." Even if, with the Darwinians, we go the length of saying that all the present and past varieties of serpents had one common progenitor, there must have been at least one pair, male and female, in Eden. Which of all the serpents, or which of the two, became the most subtil—so vastly superior to its mate and to all other serpents—in so unnatural a manner? And how did it become so? Was it created so? or how did it make itself such? If it was created "most subtil," while other serpents were created different in subtility, then the serpent race at least cannot have been created, as the Scripture expressly tells us that all animals were, "after their kind." If it afterwards became the "most subtil" of all, by what means was this done? Of itself? That is physically impossible. By God's power? Then God would have been working miracles, Himself to ruin His own work, which is absurd. By Satanic possession? That, as we shall see hereafter, does not remove all the difficulty (see Section II., p. 66).

Besides, which of all the serpents, or which of the two, became the tempter? Why did that one specially undertake that office? Above all, why is that one, above all other serpents, called "*the* Serpent"? and why is it not stated, as in this hypothesis it ought to have been, that "one of the serpents was the most subtil," instead of merely saying "*the* Serpent"? There is no reasonable answer to these questions.

2.

This special Serpent is said to have been "the most subtil of all the beasts of the field;" or rather, as I have shown from the Hebrew text, "the most intelligent of all living beings," including men, and perhaps some angels. The word "subtil," too, we have seen to mean, in the original, "intelligent, with reasoning powers." This Serpent, therefore, is declared to have been the most intelligent or rational of all living beings on the earth—more intelligent than man himself, for the text will bear that interpretation. Serpents are not, of course, intelligent with reasoning power; that is certain. But (not to insist too much on the special and peculiar meaning of Hebrew or Greek words), is it at all true, that the serpent, even in mere animal subtility or intelligence, is above all the beasts of the field? Not in the least true. Far from excelling all other animals in intelligence, it is, in fact, much inferior to many of them. This is a most important point. I say that in no reasonable sense is any bestial serpent "more subtil than all the beasts of the field." Let us examine the case in detail, for it is a crucial statement in the narrative.

Most animals can be tamed and taught and trained. They display more or less animal intelligence, in answering the calls made upon them, to learn something more than natural instinct teaches them. But neither in its natural state, nor under domestication, has the serpent any, even the slightest, claim to being considered " the most subtil of all the beasts of the field." In its natural state it is far surpassed by many animals; as, for instance, the ant, the beaver, the bee, the elephant. In a domesticated state it is simply immeasurably inferior to most other animals; as, for instance, the dog, the goat, the horse, the monkey, the elephant. It is marvellous to see what some animals are capable of being taught. But the serpent? Nothing at all! During my long sojourn of a score of years in India, I have seen hundreds of tamed serpents, of every variety and size. The same natives who train them and make a living by them, train also other animals for the same purposes. They succeed in teaching some wonderful things to these other animals:—to the serpents—nothing! The performances of these tamed serpents consist solely in erecting and waving their crests to the sound of a flageolet—and no more. And even during this poor performance, their sole object seems to be to glide away to any cover near at hand, that may suggest to them the possibility of an escape, or of a hiding-place. If there be no such cover, the serpent quietly coils himself up, and listens, with head erect, to the music. Among serpents, the cobra di capello (*Naja tripudians*), which erects its crest higher than most other serpents, does wave itself to and fro, and sometimes execute what is, by courtesy, called a "dance." It advances and recedes according as the snake-man recedes or advances. But close observation shows that this also is an unintelligent and purely instinctive motion. Never once have I seen or heard of a serpent having been successfully taught to perform any tricks, or having learned to do any actions, or of having been trained to anything more than to a passive submission (not without frequent symptoms of anger in each performance) in being exposed to public gaze, and being handled, and put around the person of the exhibitor. The so-called "fight" of these trained serpents with the munghoose (or *newla*), a kind of weasel common in India, is a mere matter of instinctive self-defence. Such fights are of frequent occurrence even in wild forest life. And besides, both in the wild and in the tamed state, the munghoose generally, almost invariably, gets the better in the fight. The only cases of defeat are when a not fully grown munghoose is pitted against an exceptionally large or vigorous serpent. I do not wish to deny, nor does my thesis require me to deny, the possibility of teaching tricks to a serpent, at the expense of very great care, skill, and patience. It is enough for the purpose of the objection which we are considering, that the serpent cannot be said to be "the most subtil of all the beasts of the field." For the ordinary care, skill, and patience, which in India are successful in teaching the goat, the monkey, and the elephant to do such strange and wonderful things, fail utterly to do as much, or anything like as much, with serpents. This alone would suffice to prove the fact that the bestial serpent is not, by any means, the "most subtil of all the beasts of the field," as the sacred narrative states that the Serpent-tempter was.

In order to ascertain yet further the alleged subtility of the serpent race, I visited the London Zoological Gardens on purpose, and spoke to one of the keepers at the snake-house, who has had an experience of over a score of years, he told me, with serpents. In answer to my question, he emphatically declared that, as a class, serpents could by no means be called intelligent animals. What intelligence they possess is of a very low type, and is confined almost exclusively to a bare recognition, in a very undemonstrative way, of the keepers who have for some time attended and fed them.

The facts of natural history, therefore, are conclusively against the bestial serpent being, in any sense, the most subtil, clever, or intelligent of all the beasts of the field. Yet, under the erroneous impression that the letter of Gen. iii. 1 required them to produce proofs of superior and surpassing intelligence in bestial serpents, even grave authors have not scrupled to put forward the most shallow and absurd reasons (if by courtesy they may be so termed) for their unnatural belief in the serpent's subtility. A mere statement, however, of these so-called reasons will suffice to show us that they deserve no serious consideration, and will excite our wonder how they were ever seriously adduced, discussed, and accepted. I proceed to place here all these so-called proofs of serpent-wisdom which I have been able to collect from various authors, most of whom go on merely repeating their predecessors' statements.

1. It is given as a proof of the serpent's wisdom or intelligence, that when it is attacked, it tries to hide its head, and seeks, above all other considerations, to keep that safe; knowing that, if its head is safe, it need not fear being killed. This conduct

reminds us of the proverbial stupidity of the ostrich, a great deal more than it gives us any specially high idea of the serpent's intelligence. This is the more evident when we consider that the head is not the only vulnerable part of a serpent's body; and that, therefore, it is not true that, the head of the serpent being safe, the life of the animal is also safe. A good blow with any instrument, whether sharp or blunt, on any part of a serpent's body except the tail, causes a lingering but certain death, by severing or crushing the spinal vertebræ, even though the head, by being hidden or kept out of harm's way, remains untouched. So, likewise, death can also be easily inflicted on a serpent, without touching its head, by any severe cutting, ripping, or biting open of the thorax, belly, or abdomen. It is thus that the munghoose generally attacks and kills the serpent, when the head is either hidden under the coils of the body, or under some other object. It is no proof, therefore, of intelligence that the serpent hides its head; just the reverse. For if it looked danger in the face and opposed it courageously, its deadly poison might often give it a victory, where it generally finds death, by hiding its head.

2. Some commentators have adduced, as a sign

of the serpent's superior intelligence, a silly tale believed in former times, that when the animal is about to drink, it first lays aside its poison-bag, to prevent the possibility of imbibing its own poison; and that, after having slaked its thirst, it replaces the bag in its mouth, to be ready for offensive or defensive purposes. I suppose no one believes this fable now; yet I have found it repeated in very modern works. The serpent has not the power of ejecting its poison gland or bag. Nor would there be any necessity for doing so. It has been long since proved, by actual experiments, that serpent-poison is innocuous in the healthy stomach, which can easily digest it; and that it does not prove fatal, except when conveyed directly into the blood, either by a bite, or through a wound or ulceration. This, therefore, even if it were true, would be no proof of superior intelligence in the serpent.

3. It is another old fable, that the serpent shows its intelligence by attacking nude men, but flying from those who are clothed, knowing that it has a less chance of killing these than the others. It is strange that some authors put it exactly the opposite way;—that the serpent avoids a nude man, but attacks one who is clothed. But this contradiction is no wonder; for when people talk of what has no

foundation in truth, it is very natural that they should fall into absurd blunders. So it is here; for the assertion is not true, as a matter of fact. Except when defending its young (as all animals do in the most ferocious way), the serpent, if it has the possibility of an escape, invariably glides away at the approach of man, or of any large animal. It never attacks them, except when hurt, or when surprised without the possibility of escape. In countries much infested with serpents, it is not an uncommon event for one of these reptiles to glide over a limb, or over the body of a man, without inflicting a bite, if the man remains still and quiet. But it is equally a common event for a bite to be inflicted, if the serpent, before it has glided quite away, be startled and frightened by any sudden, even involuntary, movement of the man. If such a movement, however, occurs immediately after the reptile has glided even a short distance, it at once seeks safety in flight, and does not attempt to return and bite the cause of its terror. Being clothed or nude has nothing to do with the matter. This instance also of the serpent's intelligence or malice is as untrue as it is inconclusive.

4. It is a very common assertion among commentators, that the serpent, full of subtle cunning

and malice, lies in stealthy ambush for man and other animals, and bites them unawares in the heel to kill them. To begin with, we are not concerned with malice, but with intelligence, of which this, of itself, would be no proof. It would, at most, be an instinctive act, like that of the lion watching for its prey. But the statement, though repeated by dozens of authors, is utterly untrue! All the facts and observations of natural history show the serpent to be a quiet, shy, retiring animal, which (as stated in the preceding paragraph, No. 3) never willingly or wilfully attacks either man or other of the larger animals. It does, of course, attack the smaller animals on which it feeds, as frogs, mice, small birds, etc. These, however, are only its natural food; and seeking that food is no sign or proof of malice, cunning, or intelligence.

5. Pliny and others give, among the instances of the intelligence and cunning of the serpent, a number of tales, presenting us with imaginary details of the manner in which it casts its skin. These tales we need not consider minutely, because those of them which are not simply untrue indicate neither intelligence nor cunning. They merely describe a natural operation, taught to the serpent by simple animal instinct.

6. Nor can the fascination which the serpent is said to exercise on the small birds and animals on which it feeds be cited as a proof of its subtility or intelligence. This is a merely natural effect, not depending on the intelligence of the serpent, but proceeding from the natural instinct of the victims. It is merely the fascination, or rather the paralysis, of fear and deadly terror. It occurs with other beasts of prey also. Nay, man himself, in certain circumstances of fear, gives way to such paralysis of the motive powers. It is the gaze of the serpent that produces this effect, which is not the result of any manœuvres or plans of the serpent. It is, therefore, no proof of superior intelligence, but only of a special instinct.

These six points exhaust the list!

There is absolutely nothing more than this put forward by any one, to prove the superior intelligence or subtility of the serpent. It does not prove it in the least degree. Nay, more. This utter and complete failure to prove the serpent to be "the most subtil of all the beasts of the field," aggravates and emphasizes the difficulty it was supposed to remove. Were it the dog, the elephant, or the monkey, how easy would it not be to prove that they possess a considerable amount of an intelligence which seems at times almost superior to mere bestial cunning and subtility, and almost approaches to reason! But nothing of the kind can be brought forward in favour of the serpent. I unhesitatingly affirm that the facts of natural history prove to a certainty that there is no possible sense in which it can be asserted with truth of any bestial serpent, that it is "the most subtil of all the beasts of the field." Yet such, the Scripture expressly tells us, was the Serpent-tempter. Therefore he could not have been the bestial serpent.

Here it may be objected by some, that our Lord Himself praises the wisdom of the serpent (Matt. x. 16), saying, "Be ye therefore wise [prudent] as serpents, and simple as doves." One may easily reply to this objection, that our Lord spoke of these two animals only as of two well-known symbols, and not of their animal natures. It was then His intention to inculcate a moral principle to guide us in our acts, and not to teach natural history. Hence He took, as illustrations of His meaning, two symbols well known to His hearers—the serpent as the symbol of prudence, and the dove as the symbol of simplicity. The serpent may be used (and he really was in ancient times) as the symbol of prudence without his being, therefore, actually wise or prudent. Was not the owl, Minerva's bird, also used as the symbol of wisdom? But does that prove that the Greeks considered the owl to be the wisest of birds? Certainly not. Again, take the other symbol here used by our Lord—the dove. The dove is not naturally simple in any sense. It is just as wide awake and alert and watchful as any other wild bird; and it is perhaps the most erotic of all animals. So much for its simplicity! The serpent is no more intelligent or prudent by nature, than the dove is simple. But they were well-known symbols in Judæa. As such our Lord used them, in their symbolic, and not in their natural, sense. Hence His words create no difficulty in the way of our holding, as is clearly proved by natural history, that the serpent is not, by any means, "the most subtil of all the beasts of the field."

If, therefore, by "the Serpent" in Gen. iii. 1, is meant a bestial serpent, the facts of natural history would be in open and direct contradiction with the words of Scripture. It is impossible to over-estimate the trenchant force of this objection, which is absolutely fatal to the commonly received interpretation, that the bestial serpent was (in any way) concerned in the temptation. The Serpent that was concerned in the temptation "was the most subtil" of all on earth; and such the bestial serpent neither is, nor ever was, nor naturally could be.

3.

A bestial serpent could not be, of himself, such a tempter as is represented in Gen. iii., talking and reasoning with Eve. He could not, of himself, have spoken with a human voice. That is a physical impossibility.

In answer to this otherwise insurmountable difficulty, we are told that "with God all things are possible," even making dumb, irrational animals speak with a human voice, as He actually caused Balaam's ass to do (see Numb. xxii. 28). But the cases are not parallel; and the almighty power of God cannot be brought forward for the explanation of Gen. iii. We all admit, of course, the almighty power of God; and that He could, if He chose to exercise that power, cause even a bestial serpent to speak and reason for a time. This He did in the case of Balaam's ass. But this animal was caused to speak, in order to prevent Balaam from further resisting the will of God. The serpent, in the other case, would have been caused to speak, in order directly to excite Eve to sin against God's express command. God would thus have been working a stupendous miracle, against His own command, and in order to cause a breach of that command. This is simply absurd. He would, moreover, have become, in this way, the direct author of moral evil, the direct agent Himself of the temptation. This is opposed to the Scripture: "God tempteth no one" (James i. 13). The reply, therefore, which urges the almighty power of God as the means of the temptation, fails to solve the difficulty; and it remains in its full force.

4.

The sacred narrative represents Eve as entering into a rational conversation with "the Serpent," without showing any sign of surprise or alarm. If "the Serpent" was a bestial one, such conduct would have been both foolish and unnatural.

It is true that the world was yet young, and that experience was still but small. Adam and Eve, however, had been created in the full perfection of man and woman-hood, of both body and mind. They knew that they were the only two human beings in Paradise; the only two rational animals among the innumerable species of animals, over which power and dominion had been given to them, by the common Creator. This is evident from Gen. i. 27, 28, compared with Gen. ii. 18–22. The other animals had even been brought by God to Adam, who had given to each its appropriate name. All this Eve knew well. She was aware that these animals did not talk with a human voice, an articulate speech, and rational arguments. She would, therefore, have been naturally much surprised and alarmed at such voice, speech, and argument from a bestial serpent. She would naturally have gone at once to Adam, to consult with him on this preternatural phenomenon. Yet the sacred narrative represents her as doing nothing of the kind. She does not manifest the least surprise, suspicion, or alarm. On the contrary, she takes it as a matter of course. She appears to have talked and argued with "the Serpent," in the most natural and unconcerned manner; just as if she had been dealing with another rational human being. This unnatural unconcern, if "the Serpent" was a bestial serpent, can be explained only on the supposition of a silliness and folly in Eve, utterly incompatible with the perfection of that state in which the first pair were created and placed.

In reply to this most serious objection, it has been urged, that the serpent may have stated to Eve, that it acquired the use of speech and of reason from having itself eaten of the fruit of that forbidden tree; and that this statement, together with its apparent verification, may have both conquered Eve's surprise, and prevented her having recourse to Adam.

We may at once candidly admit that this *supposition*, if it could but be proved to be a *fact*, might be considered to remove this difficulty in a plausible way; provided it were the sole difficulty attending the narrative. But it is not the sole difficulty; and the solution does not touch any others. Besides, admitting that supposition, it would still seem to most of us, that even then Eve would naturally have had good grounds for intense surprise, for deep reflection, and for immediate consultation with Adam. But however that may be, the great and fatal flaw in this reply,—as in all these theories —is that it is, simply and purely, a mere gratuitous supposition. It has no foundation in the sacred narrative. We find not a single word in Gen. iii. of such a statement having been made by the Serpent. We are not allowed, in the interpretation of Scripture, to make such gratuitous suppositions without good grounds in the text itself; and here none are to be found. A difficulty which requires nothing short of so groundless a supposition to meet it, may fairly be considered a very grave, nay, an absolutely insurmountable, difficulty.

5.

There is no reasonable sense in which the serpent is "cursed above all cattle, and above all beasts of the field."

If it cannot compare to advantage with the higher and nobler animals, it is itself greatly superior, in its natural condition, to many of the lower ones. It is but one of many creeping things or reptiles, and by no means the least among them. It is superior in the conformation of its body, in the rapidity of its movements, and in the keenness of its instincts, to many other similar creeping things. It is well provided with a means of defence in the noiseless swiftness of its course as a means of escape; and in its deadly poison as a means of attacking its enemies when escape is impossible. It is equally well able to provide for its food and subsistence with the best-favoured animals. In all these matters it is immeasurably superior to many of its fellow-reptiles; for instance, to the lizard, the earthworm, the frog, the snail, or the slug. It is not, therefore, the most cursed of all creatures.

In reply we are told, that the serpent is abominable to all creatures, and is most detested and avoided by all; and that, in this way, it is the most cursed of all. But, in the first place, the Scripture does not say that the serpent is to be the most abominable and detested of all creatures, but the most *cursed;* and we have no right to twist the meaning of that word to suit our theories. Being cursed, in the scriptural sense, means being made despised, abject, helpless, and miserable. This is not verified in the serpent above all other animals, as we have seen. In the next place, it is not true that there is any special natural abhorrence in all creatures towards the serpent, more than there is, for instance, towards the lion, the tiger, the alligator, the crocodile. Hence the difficulty remains; and no amount of cavilling can be made to verify this curse in the case of the bestial serpent.

6.

There is no special reciprocal enmity between the serpent tribe and man.

On the part of the serpent there is not found the

least appearance of any special enmity against man. As has been already said, the serpent is by nature a shy and timorous animal. He never goes in quest of man, or lies in wait for him, or attacks him, or longs to kill him, any more than he does for other larger animals—that is to say, not at all. When it is possible, he avoids man and seeks to fly from his presence, having this trait in common with most wild animals. Nay; wolves, tigers, lions, and some other animals, have a far greater, intenser, and more active enmity against man—if that can, properly speaking, be called an enmity, which is but the result of mere animal instinct. These animals, according to their nature, do attack man, either openly or by stealth, and fight him often not unsuccessfully, when hunted. Hence the enmity against man on the part of the serpent is conspicuous by its absence, or is certainly much less than that which certain other animals bear to man.

Neither can it be truthfully asserted that man has any special enmity against the serpent tribe. He kills serpents, it is true, wherever he can find them, because they are a danger to his life. But this is no sign of any special enmity; for he does the same equally, and for the same reason, to many other animals; for instance, to the scorpion, the lion, the tiger, the wolf, the bear, the eagle, the alligator. Nay, more. Man shows a far greater antagonism against some other wild animals than against the serpent; say, for instance, the larger animals of the feline race. For man never goes in quest of the serpent to kill it, though he invariably tries to kill it when he meets it. But he does actually go in quest of the larger animals, for the express purpose of killing them, besides killing them when he happens to meet them. In some countries, man has waged a war of extermination against some specially obnoxious animals; as, for instance, in England against wolves. But when or where has such a war been ever waged against serpents? The apparent hatred, therefore, of man against serpents is not a special enmity; it is merely his common natural enmity against all wild noxious animals. Nor, on the other hand, as we have shown, has the serpent any special enmity against man. Hence this clause also of the curse upon "the Serpent" is not at all verified in the case of the bestial serpent; and this fact constitutes another insuperable difficulty against the generally received theory.

7.

Condemning a bestial serpent to "go on its belly" is not a curse or punishment, in any reasonable sense of the words. Going on its belly is, and always was, and must, of its essential nature, always be the ordinary mode of progression of the serpent. Whether there were or were not, both before and since the curse, other animals with serpentine bodies, having wings or feet, and hence called flying or crawling serpents, is foreign to the question in hand. Such would have retained their previous forms. The text of Gen. iii. does not speak of such flying or crawling serpents; nor does it say that by the curse the serpent lost its pristine form and mode of progression, or its wings and feet, and had thereafter to go on its belly. This would be another of the many gratuitous suppositions made to maintain this theory, and as such it is clearly inadmissible. Such animals could not be called simply "the Serpent," as we have it in Gen. iii. The text indicates generically the ordinary serpent, by its own nature a glider on its belly; made originally and meant to progress by undulatory, contractive and expansive movements of its spinal column, aided by the leverage of the pectoral and abdominal ribs and scales. To an animal so created, movement on its belly is its sole natural movement; and the condemnation in the text becomes simply meaningless. Torture the text as you please, going on its belly is no more a punishment, in any reasonable sense, to a serpent, than walking is to a horse, flying to an eagle, or swimming to a shark.

The reply of commentators is a hackneyed one—that this mode of progression, natural to the serpent before the curse, was by that curse made a punishment. This, however, is a mere play upon words. It means nothing. It has no definite sense. What is natural cannot become a real curse, under the circumstances here narrated, in any reasonable sense.

But (the commentators reply) labour is man's natural condition, and death his natural end on this earth;—yet they are part of Adam's curse. Childbearing in pain is the natural lot of woman;—yet it is also part of Eve's curse. The rainbow, as a natural phenomenon, existed before the Flood;—yet it was afterwards made the covenant of God with man against a future deluge.

But these instances are only apparently, and not really, to the point. They are easily disposed of.

Adam had been raised to a state far above what his mere nature demanded. In that state he was not required to labour, and he would have been preserved from death. The curse cast him back to natural labour and death; and these, though natural to man, became a real evil after his sin, and in punishment of it. For it entailed the loss of greater excellence once enjoyed. The same applies to the case of Eve. The difference between their cases and that of the serpent is, therefore, vast. He had not been once raised to a higher state, from which a degradation back to his own natural state could be a punishment. He always went on his belly. He was created such as to necessitate his doing so. He was not first so created, and then, after having been endowed with a higher mode of locomotion, cast back to be a creeping thing. Therefore his curse can in no manner be compared with that of Adam and Eve; and it still remains true, that what is natural cannot (of itself, and independently of past supernatural favours, such as are not claimed in the case of the serpent) be a curse in any reasonable sense. For Adam and Eve the curse was indeed a real one, entailing a real degradation and punishment. To the serpent it was no punishment at all, and no degradation. It took away nothing; it changed nothing; it lowered nothing.

Nor does the instance of the rainbow in any way help the upholders of this theory. It is, of course, physically certain that the rainbow existed before the Flood. It is equally certain, from the Scriptures, that it was afterwards very appropriately and beautifully indicated by God to Noah to be His covenant with man, that He would never again destroy the world by water; with which that rainbow has physically so intimate and necessary a connection—though then and for ages afterwards, men knew it not. God gave;— in this case, a pre-existent phenomenon, often repeating itself at heavy downfalls of rain, as the sign of His resolution for the future. But the condemnation of the serpent is palpably quite a different thing. Its going on its belly is not, in Gen. iii., to be a sign of anything else. It is simply condemned (and, according to this hypothesis, not for any fault of its own, but for the fault of quite a different being) to go on its belly, for always. Such a condemnation, in the case of the bestial serpent, would be as absurd as if God had condemned water, under the well-known physical circumstances, to produce a rainbow, as a punishment on the water, for having been God's instrument in destroying the world. To establish a parallel with the case of the serpent, we should have to change the words of the covenant, and make God address the water in some such terms: "And because thou hast but lately drowned the world, thou shalt be punished by having to refract the rays of the sun, and to produce rainbows till the end of time." How absurd it sounds when thus expressed! The reply, therefore, that what was natural before was afterwards changed into a punishment, is in reality a sound without any rational meaning, and is simply ridiculous and unworthy of serious consideration.

8.

There is no reasonable sense in which it is verified of the serpent, "Dust shalt thou eat all the days of thy life."

Dust neither is nor can be, in any reasonable sense, the food of the serpent, or indeed of any other animal. That this is a physical impossibility, is demonstrated by chemistry. Dust is not a nutritive substance. Some travellers, it is true, have spoken of the existence, in some remote countries, of a certain kind of clay which is eaten, and is possessed of some nutritive properties. But an analysis would certainly show that this clay does not nourish, *inasmuch as it is dust*, but because it happens to contain some digestible ingredients mixed with it in quantities sufficient for nutritive purposes. It is not of such clay—very rarely found, even if its existence be not a mere travellers' tale—that the sacred narrative speaks. It speaks of common, ordinary dust, as dust. This is physically indigestible, and incapable of assimilation with animal bodies.

The explanations attempted by commentators are various. The older adhere to the strict letter, and maintain, in spite of chemistry and natural history, that serpents do feed on dust. The more modern commerttators satisfy themselves, though not their readers, by asserting that the serpent, as a creeping thing, having its mouth close to the ground, off which it takes its food, must necessarily eat a great quantity of dust with that food, and thus verify the letter of the curse. If this, however, were the manner in which the curse is verified; and if "dust" were "eaten" by the serpent taking its food off the ground, then all animals (except fishes, a few birds, and the quadrumana) would be equally eaters of dust with the serpent; and this would, therefore, be no special or peculiar curse on the serpent. But in reality a very little observation of the habits of animals will suffice to show us that, by instinctive movements of their lips, they succeed naturally in keeping off dust from their food, to a far greater extent than will be believed by the unobservant. But, even granting that much dust is thus swallowed by the serpent, we remain just where we were before. This also must have occurred before the curse; for the serpent even then naturally crept on its belly, with its mouth close to the ground. This also would be a natural habit of the serpent; and therefore (as seen above in No. 7) it could not have become, in any true sense, a curse or punishment.

With regard to the older commentators and their statements that serpents do eat dust as food, I think "every schoolboy knows" that they do not; and that their food consists, as naturalists tells us, of insects, reptiles, and small birds and animals, which they catch, swallow, and digest, much as other animals do. The serpent has no special organs for digesting or assimilating dust. It is carnivorous and insectivorous.

It is not, therefore, a fact that the serpent uses dust as an article of food. That some dust is swallowed involuntarily with its food is common to the serpent with most other animals, and is natural to it. This must also have occurred before the curse. It cannot, therefore, in any reasonable sense, be a curse. This is, therefore, another clause of the curse, which is absolutely inapplicable to the bestial serpent.

9.

"The Serpent" is not stated to have come to Eve or to have gone away from her, as should have been said of a corporeal being. Again, God seeks Adam and Eve, corporeal beings, when He comes to pass sentence upon them. But there is no search for the Serpent. Yet when God punishes with His curse the violation of His commands, there the Serpent is:—suddenly present again on the scene, in the very hiding-place of his victims; and again he is not said to have come or gone away. Now, is it not highly improbable that, even after that melancholy opening of the eyes of Adam and Eve, the bestial serpent, if that had been the tempter, would have been permitted by the guilty pair to accompany them in their flight, and to share their retreat?

10.

A bestial serpent, being an irrational and therefore not a free agent, could incur no moral guilt in its acts. Even if it could by any possibility have, of itself, perpetrated that temptation, it could not sin in doing so. Therefore, in justice, it did not deserve any punishment, and should not have been cursed. But "the Serpent" was cursed; hence "the Serpent" was not the bestial serpent.

11.

God said to "the Serpent" (ver. 15) that the Seed of the woman was to bruise that Serpent's head. Mark well the words ;—to bruise the head of that one identical Serpent, the tempter, which was then being cursed; not the head of his seed. True that an enmity was to be placed between the woman and the Serpent, as also between her Seed and his seed. But her Seed, the future Redeemer —Jesus Christ—was to bruise the head of that particular Serpent;—and that same Serpent was to bruise His heel. "I will place an enmity (1) between thee and the woman; and (2) between thy seed and her seed; (3) *He* shall bruise *thy* head, and (4) *thou* shalt bruise *His* heel." This bruising, as all Christians believe, took place on the day of the crucifixion and death of our Lord Jesus Christ. That identical Serpent, therefore, the tempter, was to be still living, to see that day—over four thousand years after the curse! It is evident that no bestial serpent, living in Eden at the time of the Fall, could continue living till the coming of the Redeemer. The object, therefore, of this curse could not be a mere bestial serpent.

12.

Intimately connected with the foregoing objection is the present one. Our Lord physically bruised the head of no bestial serpent. Therefore the curse could not have been meant for any bestial serpent.

Nor can we admit it to be any sufficient reply to this objection, that this part of the curse was metaphorical; because the rules of correct interpretation do not allow us, in the same sentence, to change about from the literal to the metaphorical sense, and back again at will. Besides, what is the meaning of a metaphorical bruising of a bestial serpent's head? None; again words are being used without any definite meaning. If it be said that "the Serpent" here (and not the bruising) is a metaphorical one, I say that we cannot admit two serpents where there is only the one serpent—the tempter—mentioned all through the sacred narrative; and if in this part "the Serpent" is metaphorical, metaphorical he must be all through.

This theory of metaphorical interpretation we have seen to be untenable.

13.

With regard to the going on the belly and to the eating of dust, we must particularly notice that the condemnation, all through the narrative, is in the singular number, addressed solely to that one serpent which tempted Eve: "Cursed art *thou*," "on *thy* belly shalt *thou* go," "dust shalt *thou* eat all the days of *thy* life," "bruise *thy* head." While the "enmity" is extended to the seed, all the other clauses of the curse are confined to that one individual serpent. What then happened to its mate; and to the other serpents, if any, then in Eden? Were they blessed or cursed? How did they go? What did they eat? If they shared in these natural operations, turned by the curse into a punishment, how could it be just to make them share in the punishment, although they had

had no share whatever in the temptation? If, on the other hand, it was no punishment for them, how was it one for that serpent? If they did not "go on their bellies" or "eat dust," then what did they do? Would there not be a most unnatural anomaly for one serpent to be leading one kind of life, and all others (including its mate) a different kind of life? Whichever way we view it, the difficulty is insoluble.

These are the principal difficulties attending the interpretation of Gen. iii., which holds that the bestial serpent was the means of the temptation of Eve.

SECTION II.—*Difficulties attending the Bestial Serpent having been possessed by Satan.*

If to the serpent having been the means of the fall, we superadd that it was seized upon and possessed by Satan, then we superadd the following to the foregoing difficulties:—

1.

That Satan took possession of the serpent and used it as an instrument for the temptation, is a purely gratuitous supposition, which, as we have seen, has no foundation in one single word of the sacred narrative. It is, therefore, plainly inadmissible.

2.

Satan is not even once mentioned in any part of that narrative, neither explicitly nor implicitly. There is only "the Serpent." Supposing a bestial serpent to have been present, and seeing that the sacred narrative does not tell us of the presence of any third party, but only of Eve and the Serpent, it surely thus leaves no room whatsoever for Satan in this supposition.

3.

If the bestial serpent was used by the superior power of Satan without any voluntary co-operation of its own, for the deception of Eve, it would have been so used without any moral fault of its own. Nay, without even any material fault of its own; for it was not itself at all the real agent; but at most it was only a passive and entirely innocent instrument of another's malignity. Is it compatible with the justice of God to inflict so heavy a curse on an entirely innocent instrument, and to take no cognizance of the really guilty agent? The cases in Lev. xx. 15, 16 are not to the point; because death is there decreed not so much as a punishment on the beast, as the means of preventing a repetition of the acts; and of those acts the animals had been the real active agents, and not merely the passive instruments.

4.

If by "the Serpent" we are to understand (according to the commonly received theory) the bestial serpent acted upon for a time by Satan, then the same bestial serpent must have been the subject of the curse. Only three are cursed— Adam, Eve, and "the Serpent." Satan, therefore, who in this theory is the most guilty of all, escapes without any curse or punishment whatsoever, although, as the most guilty, his punishment should have been the heaviest of all.

5.

If "the Serpent" was a bestial serpent temporarily possessed and used by Satan to seduce Eve, then, the seduction having been effected, and the sin of Adam and Eve having been completed when both had eaten of the forbidden fruit, that possession must have ceased as soon as its object was accomplished. The serpent, therefore, must have become free from that possession. It was then no longer anything except a mere bestial serpent. Yet God addresses, and curses the poor bestial serpent, even after the Satanic possession had ceased, as if it had been the real agent of a deed, done under entirely different circumstances, which had ceased, and as if it were responsible for that deed, as under this hypothesis it neither was nor could be. "Because thou [bestial serpent, according to this theory] hast done this," said God; when as a matter of fact the poor beast had done nothing at all, and when the assumed connection between it and Satan, the real agent, had ceased for ever. Is it not the height of absurdity to represent God acting as this theory makes Him?

6.

Whether we consider "the Serpent" as acting under Satanic coercion or by itself, the argument drawn from the absence in the sacred narrative, of any surprise on the part of Eve at the serpent speaking and reasoning, still holds good. For to her it would still have been but an irrational animal, acting preternaturally as a rational human being. What can she have known of Satanic possession?

These difficulties, superadded to most of those already given in the preceding section (especially the inapplicability of the curse), attend the theory of a Satanic possession and coercion of a bestial serpent for the purpose of tempting Eve. No successful attempts have been made to furnish a reasonable answer to any of these difficulties. Every reply ever attempted has been met, as we have seen, and refuted without much trouble or waste of ingenuity.

All these difficulties (each one in itself being of much individual weight) form, when taken all together, a cumulative argument so strong as to render perfectly hopeless the attempt to overturn it. I lay special stress upon the indubitable fact, that not a fragment of these theories can be founded on a literal understanding of the sacred narrative, without bringing in the support of a series of suppositions, which are purely gratuitous, and have not the least suggestion of them in the text. There is not a single clause regarding "the Serpent" which fits in with what we know, from natural history, of the nature of a bestial serpent. There is not a single clause which does not furnish a special difficulty and objection of its own, against the supposition that a bestial serpent tempted Eve, with or without Satanic possession and coercion.

It is not in any of these theories, therefore, that we must seek for a correct and satisfactory explanation of this most important narrative. We must look elsewhere for "the Serpent"-tempter. Whoever he was, he certainly was not a bestial serpent, nor any one using a bestial serpent as his instrument. These suppositions are merely gratuitous, and are attended with insoluble difficulties.

CHAPTER V.

OBJECTIONS AGAINST PROPOSING A NEW THEORY.

THE difficulties which have been shown to attend every one of the theories hitherto used for an explanation of the temptation of Eve by "the Serpent," leave the question still very mysterious, and still open for a satisfactory solution.

I purpose, without actually condemning the commonly propounded and, doubtless, well-meant theories, to argue (as against unbelievers only) that there is yet remaining a literal sense—and the only really literal sense—in which the Scripture narrative, of the temptation and fall of man and the subsequent curse on the Serpent, can be rationally held, without admitting any unnatural apparition, or any Satanic possession of a bestial serpent, or any conversation with Eve in a human manner by a bestial serpent. If this can but be proved, and such an explanation be given, the narrative would be at once freed from all improbabilities and difficulties, and be rendered impregnable against infidel and rationalistic attacks. And yet the faithful would still be left at full liberty to choose whatever interpretation might best suit the taste and mind of each individual.

Here, however, I must answer, in anticipation, two objections that may be raised, with some plausibility, against my proposed undertaking.

I.

It may be argued that I am needlessly abandoning the literal and natural sense of the sacred narrative, and flying to a figurative sense.

This, if true, would indeed be a grave objection; but it is not true.

I might reply that this is one of those cases in which, if even a novel figurative sense were sought for, it could not be said that such a search was a needless one. This is proved by the very existence of the numerous and insurmountable difficulties which, as we have seen, attend the sacred narrative, when taken in the sense in which it has been commonly interpreted. But that is not my chief reply. My principal answer to the objection is, that I am not at all abandoning the real literal sense. I abandon only the common interpretation of the text, which I have already shown to be by no means a literal one. On the contrary, it has been shown to be a pure supposition, completely opposed to the letter of the sacred narrative. I purpose to substitute for it a very literal interpretation, which shall be a truly literal sense, instead of being only a pretended literal one. I am not going to maintain that there was no serpent concerned in the temptation; or that "the Serpent" is a metaphorical, or figurative, or allegorical expression for something else. I shall hold that "the Serpent" did tempt Eve, and was really cursed for having done so. I shall hold all the facts as related in the sacred narrative to be literally true, as a plain historical narrative of facts. The point at issue is not whether the literal sense is not preferable to any figurative sense. I admit that it is so. The real question is, Which *is* the really literal sense? Who *is* this serpent, in a literal sense, without any gratuitous suppositions, inadmissible by the sacred text?

II.

Catholics may, moreover, urge against me, that if I deny that the temptation of Eve was effected by Satan, by his taking possession of a bestial serpent, or, in other words, under the appearance of a bestial serpent, then I shall be going against the *communem sententiam*, and consequently against the express prohibition of the Holy Council of Trent (Sess. IV.).[1]

But to this I answer that new objections must necessarily be met by new replies; that varying circumstances, of time and of increased knowledge, change the old grounds of polemics; that new theories may, and should, be advanced (with due submission to the judgment of Holy Mother Church) in order to strengthen the cause of truth against modern educated unbelief.

This has already been done, with much advan-

---

[1] The decree of the Council of Trent forbids the private interpretation of Holy Scripture, "in rebus fidei et morum, ad ædificationem doctrinæ Christianæ pertinentium." The *manner*, however, of the temptation of Eve cannot be said to belong to this category. It also forbids the private interpretation of Holy Scripture, "contra unanimem consensum Patrum." I do not think that, amid the various theories proposed, any one of them can be said to have in its favour the "*unanimem* consensum." We are, therefore, left free in this matter by the decree of the Council of Trent.

tage and success, in the case of two parallel questions, regarding two other narratives in this very Book of Genesis. I mean the Days of Creation, and the Universality of the Deluge. The acknowledged and as yet unanswered difficulties attending the narrative in Gen. iii. fully justify me in trying a new and, as I hope, a better solution. This may blamelessly be attempted, provided that I do not contemptuously condemn other theories, and provided I duly submit my judgment in all matters of faith (as I hereby most humbly, sincerely, and completely do beforehand) to the supreme authority of the Holy Catholic Church, and of its supreme head and teacher on earth, the Vicar of our Lord Jesus Christ.

CHAPTER VI.

THE NEW THEORY.

THE real question at issue, as I have said, is, What Being is indicated in Gen. iii. by the words "the Serpent"? A certain real "Serpent," of course; but what serpent?

We have already shown that we cannot reconcile with the sacred narrative, either that the bestial serpent was itself the tempter, or that Satan used it under his personal possession for this purpose, or that he assumed the apparition of one for this end. If, then, "the Serpent" in Gen. iii. was not a merely bestial serpent, nor a possessed serpent, nor an apparitional serpent, what "Serpent" was it?

The question may, in a different form, be finally put thus: Is there, besides the bestial serpent, any other Serpent mentioned in the Scriptures?—any other Serpent whose existence is proved from the Scriptures themselves;—and whose nature, as related in those very Scriptures, fits into the narrative of Gen. iii.,—who has a just title to being, *par excellence*, called "*the* Serpent"?

Yes: there is such a scriptural Serpent, distinct from the bestial one.

Several passages of Scripture exhibit before us a certain Serpent, who is also called by various other titles. This Serpent, though not a bestial serpent, is still a real Serpent. He is described in the Scriptures as being of such a nature as to have been most naturally the primary and sole agent in the temptation of Eve. His claim to being "the Serpent" of Gen. iii. can be established without any unnatural circumstances of fact, without any insurmountable difficulties of interpretation, especially without any violation of the natural and literal sense of Scripture, and without the use of any gratuitous suppositions.

In fact, "THE SERPENT" is one of the special scriptural titles of the great arch-rebel angel, Satan. This is the key to the true interpretation of Gen. iii.

This key is found in the Apocalypse (or Revelation) xii. 7, 8, and 9, where this chief leader of the rebel angels is thus spoken of:—

"7. And there was war[1] in heaven: Michael and his angels fought against[2] the dragon; and the dragon fought and his angels,

"8. And[3] prevailed not; neither was their place found any more in heaven.

"9. And the great dragon[4] was cast out, that old Serpent,[5] called[6] the[7] Devil, and Satan,[8] which deceiveth[9] the whole world:[10] he was cast out into[11] the earth, and his angels were cast out[12] with him."

This passage of holy writ pointedly refers to Gen. iii. The words, "the Serpent, he of old," as the Greek text has it, and the words, "who causes to go astray the whole world," both directly indicate the fall of the human race in our first parents. They attribute that fall to the being who is here described in Rev. xii. This being is

[1] Douay Version, "a great battle;" πόλεμος.
[2] D.V., "with."
[3] D.V., "and they."
[4] D.V., "that great dragon;" ὁ δράκων, ὁ μέγας.
[5] D.V., "the old serpent;" ὁ ὄφις, ὁ ἀρχαῖος, literally, "the serpent, he of old."
[6] D.V., "who is called;" ὁ καλούμενος.
[7] There is no "the" in the Greek text. [8] Greek, "the Satan."
[9] D.V., "who seduceth;" ὁ πλανῶν, "causes to go astray or to wander."
[10] D.V., "earth;" τὴν οἰκουμένην ὅγην, "the whole habitable earth."
[11] D.V., "unto;" εἰς.
[12] D.V., "thrown down."

called the Great Dragon, the Serpent of old. Dragon and Serpent are synonymous in Scripture and ancient natural history; a dragon being simply an older, greater, and mightier serpent among other serpents. This same being is also called Devil and Satan. It is not the Devil and Satan, who is also called the Serpent. Just the reverse. It is "the Serpent," who is also called "Devil and Satan." We are therefore compelled to conclude, that "the Serpent" is the primary name of this being; and that the Devil and Satan are only his secondary names.

Now, there is absolutely no doubt possible as to the personality of him who is here described in Rev. xii. A portion of the angels of God, here said to have been one-third of the whole, fell from their high estate, headed by a leader, who is primarily called "the Serpent," and variously and equally named Lucifer, Satan, and the Devil. And this being is not only called "the Serpent," but he is expressly called ὁ ὄφις, ὁ ἀρχαῖος—"the Serpent, he of old." This leader, therefore, of the rebel angels, in this passage of Scripture is clearly and distinctly and expressly identified with that Serpent of olden times, the deceiver of the human race from all time, whose first dealings with the human race are recorded in Gen. iii. He and he alone is the Serpent-tempter of Eve. He and he alone is the Serpent of Eden. "The Serpent" is simply one of his many scriptural titles or names.

The true interpretation of Gen. iii. consequently requires no aid of any bestial serpent at all; and "the Serpent," interchangeable with "Dragon" or "Great Serpent," is only a plain literal scriptural expression for the Devil, Satan, or Lucifer.

I do not assert positively that "the Serpent" is the sole and individual name of precisely the leader of the rebel angels. What do we really know as to whether each of the multitudinous angels, both good and bad, has or has not an individual name? "The Serpent" may or may not be an individual name; it may or may not be a common or generic name for many evil spirits. This does not affect the argument in the least. For even if "the Serpent" be only a generic or common name for many, so also is "Devil" (Διάβολος, the Calumniator) and "Satan" (שָׂטָן, the Adversary). Whatever may be held as to individual names, it is certain that this text (Rev. xii. 9) clearly and conclusively proves that "the Serpent" is one of the scriptural titles or names of the great leader of rebel spirits, and is literally equivalent to and interchangeable with "Satan," or with "Devil."

But Rev. xii. 9 is by no means a solitary passage of the Scriptures upon which I am trying to build up a new interpretation of Gen. iii. There are many other passages to the same effect. In sacred Scripture, in fact, Satan is repeatedly called "the Serpent."

Take Job xxvi. The holy sufferer eloquently mentions some of the greatest phenomena of nature, and some of the mightiest works of God.

"7. He stretcheth out the north over the empty place, and hangeth the earth upon nothing.

"8. He bindeth up the waters in His thick clouds; and the cloud is not rent under them.

"9. He holdeth back the face of His throne, and spreadeth His cloud upon it.

"10. He hath compassed the waters with bounds, until the day and the night come to an end.

"11. The pillars of heaven tremble, and are astonished at His reproof.

"12. He divideth the sea with His power; and by His understanding He smiteth through the proud.

"13. By His Spirit He hath garnished the

heavens; *and His hand hath formed the crooked Serpent.*

"14. Lo, these are parts of His ways; but how little a portion is heard of Him? but the thunder of His power who can understand?"

I hold that in ver. 13, by "the garniture of the heavens," are meant, not the inanimate stars, but the angels of heaven. This is proved by a comparison with Ps. xxxiii. (in the Douay Bible, Ps. xxxii.) 6, "By the word of the Lord the heavens were made; and all the host of them by the breath of His mouth." The expression "breath of His mouth" indicates the creation of living and rational hosts; for in Gen. ii. 7 also, God "breathed into his nostrils the breath of life, and man became a living soul." In this enumeration of the mighty works of God, therefore, ver. 13 is devoted to a description of the angels; and among the angels, as another notable instance of the almighty power of God, Job names one sole brute animal—" His hand hath formed the crooked Serpent." "Crooked" is not merely used to indicate the winding of a serpent. The word is repeatedly used in Scripture to mean *perverse* or *wicked*. Deut. xxxii. 5, "they are a crooked generation;" Ps. cxxv. (Douay, cxx.), 'crooked ways;" Phil. ii. 13, "a crooked nation."

This special crooked Serpent, therefore, is a specially perverse and wicked being, called the Serpent. Now, from the context, it is evident that Job desired to indicate the power of God as shown by His works. Among these works he mounts from the greater physical wonders of creation (he omits even man) to the wonderful existence of the angels, or (if you do not admit the parallel from the Psalms) to the marvels of the starry heavens; and he ends his catalogue with the creation of the crooked Serpent! Now, the bestial serpent race has no possible claim whatever to being ranked among the chief works of God, much less to being the apex of the whole, the most sublime of all God's works. But such precisely is Satan, the devil, the old Serpent. Here, therefore, Job distinctly and clearly names Satan under his scriptural title of "the Serpent."

So, too, Isaiah (xxvii. 1) speaks of one particular great Serpent, which the Lord will punish on the day that He punishes the iniquity of the earth: xxvi. 21, "For, behold, the Lord cometh out of His place to punish the inhabitants of the earth for their iniquity: the earth also shall disclose her blood, and shall no more cover her slain."

xxvii. 1, "In that day the Lord, with His sore,

and great, and strong sword, shall punish Leviathan that piercing Serpent, even Leviathan that crooked Serpent, and He shall slay the Dragon that is in the sea."

The punishment of this one particular Serpent is the culminating point of the anger and justice of God. The context precludes the possibility of its referring to any bestial serpent. The word "crooked" connects this text with the preceding one given from Job; and the juxtaposition of the terms "Dragon" and "Serpent" seems to connect it with Rev. xii. 9.

Again, let us open Isa. lxv. Here the prophet typifies the greatness and glory of the Church. In ver. 25 he says, "The wolf and the lamb shall feed together, and the lion shall eat straw like the bullock: *and dust shall be the Serpent's meat.*" This conclusion, with its special marked reference to Gen. iii. 14, makes it impossible to doubt that the prophet was not thinking of any bestial serpent, but of that old Serpent—Satan—the sole agent in the temptation of Eve. To interpret this text of a bestial serpent would be to thrust the serpent into a prominence noways compatible with its natural place in the creation. Besides, when the other animals are represented as having changed their natural habits, clearly showing the presence of a metaphorical sense, it follows naturally that the serpent here indicated is not the mere bestial serpent, but some other Serpent.

In Rev. (Apocalypse) xx. 2, an angel of God "laid hold on the dragon, that old Serpent [again ὁ ὄφις, ὁ ἀρχαῖος, 'the Serpent, he of old'], which is the Devil, and Satan, and bound him for a thousand years." And, in the already cited chapter (xii.), the words "Satan," "Devil," "Serpent," and "Dragon" are repeatedly used, both simultaneously and interchangeably, for one and the same person. This person is identified as the leader of the rebel angels, and, by being indicated as the enemy of the seed of the woman, is also identified as the Serpent-tempter in Gen. iii.

From these texts, it is evident that the sacred Scripture makes special and frequent mention of a certain Serpent, also the leader of the rebel angels, one of the chief of God's mightiest works; and it speaks of him under the name or title of "the Serpent." The Scripture speaks of him, in these cases, in his own individual personality, unconnected with any apparition or possession of a bestial Serpent. Yet it calls him simply "the Serpent," as in Gen. iii. It is evident, therefore, that "the

Serpent" is simply one of his scriptural names. Satan is "the Serpent," and "the Serpent" is Satan. The words are interchangeable. They mean the same person.

I hold that, under the name of "the Serpent," Gen. iii. makes as literal and direct a mention of the same leader of rebel angels, as do the other texts here cited; and that it mentions him equally in his own individual personality, unassociated with any bestial possession or apparition, as these texts do. It speaks of him simply under one of his well-ascertained scriptural titles. In Gen. iii. the words "the Serpent" are literally meant for "Satan," and for "Satan" alone, just as they are in Job xxvi., with no reference whatsoever to any connection with a bestial serpent.

In consequence, we may, throughout the whole scriptural narrative of the temptation and fall of man, safely substitute the word "Satan" for the words "the Serpent" without doing any violence to the text, or putting any construction upon it opposed to its literal sense, or making any unwarranted suppositions. Literally true it will still remain that "the Serpent" was the tempter; only it will have been proved that by "the Serpent" is simply meant Satan in his own personality. There is not only thus no *need* for any apparition or possession of a bestial serpent; there is no *room* left for either in the sacred narrative, the literal wording of which both those suppositions would violate. "The Serpent" is simply equivalent to "Satan," both being titles of the same person, and capable of being substituted for each other.

To see how completely, naturally, and perfectly this interpretation fits into the sacred narrative of Gen. iii., I proceed to repeat that narrative as we found it in the original Hebrew text, substituting the word "Satan" instead of "the Serpent;" just as in algebra we may substitute the ascertained value of an x or a y for x or y in an equation, without altering its value. I add a running commentary.

Ver. 1. "Now $\begin{Bmatrix} \text{Satan} \\ \text{the Serpent} \end{Bmatrix}$ was more subtil than any living being of the earth which the Lord God had made;" because his angelic nature and qualities, though dimmed and degraded by his fall, still constitute him superior to all animals on earth, including man, against whom principally (and not against irrational beasts) the comparison (φρονιμώ-τατος, most intelligent or thinking) is urged; for it was to cope with man that Satan came.

"And he said * unto the woman," not by any articulate audible speech, made to proceed preternaturally from the jaws of a possessed bestial serpent, or of an apparitional one; but by an internal and inaudible, yet most intelligible and soul-felt communication, of mind with mind and spirit with spirit. Thus God speaks to the heart of man with His inspirations, and our guardian angels communicate with us; and thus, too, the same Satan daily and hourly speaks to ourselves, in our various temptations. Even thus internally and inaudibly, yet quite intelligibly, Satan spoke to Eve's mind and soul. No bestial serpent, or appearance of one, was at all needed. Eve had most probably often thought over and wondered at the prohibition against the eating of that particular fruit. She had on this occasion, probably,

---

* It is scarcely necessary to point out that "to say," in Scripture, is often used in the sense of "to think," even when the thought is not expressed by audible words. A few examples must suffice. Luke iii. 8, "Do not begin to *say* [*i.e.* ' to think in yourselves '], We have Abraham for our father;" also Matt. iii. 9. Again, Matt. xvi. 7, "And they thought within themselves, *saying*." Again, Matt. xxi. 25 (Mark xi. 28; Luke xx. 2), "And they thought within themselves, *saying*." And Matt. xii. 44, of the evil spirit it is written, "Then he *saith*, I will return." In Mark v. 28, the woman with the issue of blood, who in Matt. ix. 21 "said within herself," is represented simply as saying, "For she *said*." Saying, and thinking, therefore, according to scriptural usage, are interchangeable terms where the sense may need it.

wandered near the tree, from motives of natural curiosity. Or she may have been, perhaps, moved by previous internal, indirect temptations of Satan, seemingly her own thoughts, but excited by his baleful and powerful influence, prompting her to approach and look at that wonderful tree. When she arrived there and was viewing the beautiful tree and fruit, Satan (invisibly present with her and in her, for a spirit is where it thinks) makes his first direct internal suggestion or temptation. Not through the corporeal ear, or in an audible voice caused by vibrations in the air produced from the jaws of any serpent body or apparition, but straight to the soul, by spiritual intercommunication. The serpent, Satan, therefore in this manner "said unto the woman: Strange! that God has said, Ye shall not eat of every tree of the garden!" This interjectional form of the beginning of the temptation is a matter of some importance. The temptation, in the original, is not in the interrogative form. It is not a question asked from outside; but the sentence seems much more like a thought developed in Eve's own mind, under Satanic suggestion. Satan speaks to her soul; and in her mind he causes to arise a feeling of surprise at the restraint put upon her liberty. To this thought, raised in her mind by Satan's insidious suggestion—as he daily raises similar thoughts in ourselves—Eve silently and mentally replies, as we ourselves daily argue with and reply to our own temptations.

2. "And the woman said to $\begin{Bmatrix} \text{Satan} \\ \text{the Serpent} \end{Bmatrix}$: We may eat of the fruit of the trees of the garden." And here there seems already to be a partial yielding to the influence of the temptation, in the exclusion of the phrase "of *every* tree," used by God in Gen. ii. 16. Eve already seems to consider the permission to eat "the fruit of every tree," except that one, to be so limited that she leaves out the "every." Thus she already resents the slight restriction, and despises the wide permission.

3. "But of the fruit of the tree which is in the midst of the garden, God has said, Ye shall not eat of it, neither shall ye touch it, lest perhaps ye die." The addition by Eve of the word "perhaps," which is not found in the original prohibition in Gen. ii. 17, is remarkable, as showing the increasing force of the temptation—the first glimmer of a doubt in her faith. Of this doubt Satan adroitly avails himself, and suggests a strong and open temptation against faith, against yielding

unhesitating assent to God's teaching. He enlarges the doubt into a certainty; that there is no chance of their dying; that there is no certainty in God's threat; and that it proceeds only from a jealous envy on the part of God. All this he, therefore, again communicates inaudibly to the mind of Eve as before.

4. "And {Satan the Serpent} said unto the woman, Ye shall not surely die." And he then proceeds to add another temptation. He appeals to her pride and ambition, his own favourite vices, by which he himself had fallen. He suggests to Eve a false suspicion as the reason of God's prohibition; and he finally holds out to her the false promise, that a disobedience of so arbitrary and interested a command would result in an increase of knowledge, and, in consequence, an enlargement of power, and an improvement of condition.

5. "For God knoweth that in the day ye eat thereof, then your eyes shall be opened, and ye shall be as gods, knowing good and evil." From curiosity Satan leads her to unbelief, and from unbelief to pride and ambition.

Eve dwelt with pleasure on these evil suggestions. She offered no resistance. She did not fly from the occasion of sin. She did not pray. She hesitated. She viewed the tree with a well-developed and growing desire to taste the fruit. She gazed long, perhaps, at it, till her desire for it made it seem to be "good for food," which mere sight could not tell her; and "pleasant to the eyes," which in Hebrew is "a desire unto the eyes;" and "a tree to be desired to make one wise," which also her sight could not prove, and which she had no reason to believe, except Satan's suggestion and her own longing thoughts. She yielded, and eat of it. Satan's purpose was accomplished. He ceased to act further.

We proceed to note that "the Serpent"—Satan—is not said to have come to Eve before her temptation, or to have gone away after her fall, because he is a spirit; and his coming and going are not recorded, because they did not fall under the senses. Yet they would naturally have been recorded, if a bestial serpent had been in any manner the instrument of the temptation. The Serpent-tempter is represented as being all the time present with her. Satan had been indeed really present, weaving his plot and working out his evil purpose in Eve's mind, though neither visible nor audible. He now seems to disappear for a while from the scene, and remains unnoticed in the sacred narrative. He continues still present, however, though invisible and inaudible; gloating over Eve's fall, while she eats of the fruit, and takes of it to Adam, and coaxes him to eat of it; and he does eat, and falls likewise. Still invisibly present with them, he continues to watch them, awaiting the result of his success. He watches the guilty pair, after the opening of their eyes, while they make aprons for themselves, and hear the voice of God, and hide, and are sought by Him and found, and spoken with. When the time for issuing the sentence of condemnation arrives, lo! unsought, unsummoned, this same serpent—Satan—is again on the scene, invisible yet really present, and again not mentioned as having either come or gone. How perfectly does not all this coincide with the narrative, when "the Serpent" is simply taken as another name for Satan; and how utterly it seems at variance with the commonly received theories!

Continuing still to substitute "Satan" for "the Serpent," we still find the rest of the narrative proceed rationally and intelligibly as before.

13. "And the woman said, $\begin{cases} \text{Satan} \\ \text{the Serpent} \end{cases}$ beguiled me, and I did eat.

14. "And the Lord said unto $\begin{Bmatrix} \text{Satan} \\ \text{the Serpent} \end{Bmatrix}$, Because thou hast done this," etc. These words of the curse we shall consider separately hereafter, p. 97.

When put thus, the sacred narrative, while still retaining its literal sense in the highest degree, becomes both natural and intelligible. In fact, this is the sole interpretation which retains the natural and literal sense. It needs no ingenious theories to make it probable. It presents no physical difficulties against its possibility. It holds before us the temptation and fall, both as an historical fact in its most literal sense, and also as an instructive fact for the foundation of any allegory which we may be competent to build upon it. It maintains a positive and real temptation by "a real Serpent," who is Satan himself—such a temptation as is daily experienced by ourselves. It brushes away at one stroke all cavils and sophisms, nay, all those arguments which are of some, and perhaps of great weight, against an audible temptation from a visible serpent. And yet the narrative (I repeat it, because it is of the utmost importance to be known) continues to be held in its most literal sense; substituting no metaphor, no allegory, no myth; excluding all figurative interpretation; insisting solely on the fact, proved from the Scriptures themselves, that "the Serpent" is one of Satan's scriptural names, and that by "the Serpent" in Gen. iii. Satan is meant, to the exclusion of any visible serpent. Hence no violence is done to the text, and no gratuitous supposition is adopted. The text itself is left inviolate, by substituting "Satan" for "the Serpent;" firstly, because reasons already adduced preclude the possibility of a bestial serpent having been even the instrument of the temptation; and secondly, because the Scriptures themselves tell us that Satan *is* "the Serpent, he of old." It is like substituting אֱלֹהִים for יְהוָה, Κύριος for Θεός, *Dominus* for *Deus*, or "Lord" for "God." The meaning remains the same; the sense remains the same; the person meant remains the same. This is all that we need do in Gen. iii.

CHAPTER VII.

THE CURSE ON "THE SERPENT."

I PREMISE four points for consideration, which, after what has been already seen, will easily command assent :—

1. The words of this curse are inapplicable to the bestial serpent.

2. They do not apply to any material being, and cannot, therefore, be taken in a material and literal sense.

3. If they are applicable only to a spiritual or immaterial being, they must be taken in an immaterial and spiritual sense.

4. Such an application, under the circumstances, does no violence to the letter of the sacred text.

We have now to consider the words of the curse upon the Serpent, in the light of the theory now advanced.

Ver. 14. "Because thou hast done this, cursed art

thou above every beast and above all living beings on the earth. Upon thy belly shalt thou go, and dust shalt thou eat all the days of thy life.

15. "And I will put enmity between thee and the woman, and between thy seed and her seed. It shall bruise thy head, and thou shalt bruise his heel."

Such are the words of the curse on "the Serpent."

If, putting aside the prejudices naturally caused in us by the teaching of our earliest days, we dispassionately examine the words of this curse, we shall be compelled to acknowledge that there is not one single clause in the text which can in any imaginable way be naturally applicable to a bestial serpent: cursing an apparition is, of course, too glaring an absurdity to need any examination. We have seen the ingenious theories built up, and the bold assertions made, in order to show how the curse could work on a bestial serpent. They all leave untouched the question why at all the serpent, sinless by nature, because irrational, should have been cursed. They are all, besides, more or less improbable in themselves, and opposed to real facts. Yet these theories and assertions have been copied by one author or commentator from his predecessors, till quite a literature of nonsense (I speak with all due reverence) has grown up around the subject. But it has all been in vain. The facts of natural history are too stubborn to be bent to the aid of distorted theories and tortured interpretations.

We have already seen that the bestial serpent is by no manner of means the most accursed of all animals. It does, it is true, go upon its belly; but it must have done so from the beginning, and it shares this natural mode of progression with many other animals. Unless this is equally a curse on them, it cannot be any special curse on the serpent. It does not eat dust as food. If in taking its natural food it does receive some dust into its stomach with that food, this also is natural to it, with other animals, and therefore cannot be a curse on the serpent above all other animals. There is no special enmity between the serpent and man—nay, considerably less than there is between man and some other wild and savage animals. The curse, therefore, is absolutely meaningless when it is applied to the bestial serpent; thus rendering it impossible that the bestial serpent could have been the Serpent-tempter in any sense. Not one single clause fits the bestial serpent.

But if we consider this curse as having been

passed upon Satan—"the Serpent, he of old"—then every clause assumes a definite and appropriate meaning, consonant both with the nature of things, and with numerous other passages of Holy Scripture. Let us consider it in detail in this sense, and we shall easily realize its full and true signification.

Satan is indeed cursed above every beast and above all living beings of the earth. For while they serve God, each according to his nature, and thus fulfil the end of their creation, and have an attainable object for their existence, Satan has fallen away for ever from his end. As a useless branch, he has been cut off and cast into the fire. As a sickly one out of the flock, he has been sentenced to eternal death. His punishment is made greater than that of all others, because he was the first originator and cause of all evil. This casting away, this living death, this complete degradation and punishment, have thrown him down, and lowered him beneath even the beasts of the field. He has forfeited his original end; and the object he now strives at,—to resist and oppose God,—he cannot possibly obtain; for God is Almighty.

"On thy belly shalt thou go, and dust shalt thou

eat all the days of thy life." Satan, being an incorporeal spirit, has no corporeal belly on which to go, in a literal sense; and as he requires no material sustenance, he neither eats dust nor any other food, in a literal sense. We find, however, on examination, that these two expressions have a very definite and special sense and meaning in the Holy Scriptures. The two clauses, through insensible gradations and through various shades of meaning, merge into the one idea, which in scriptural usage is most applicable to the case of Satan's condemnation in consequence of his evil deed. Going, sitting, lying, and grovelling in dust and ashes, or on the earth; prostrating, placing one's body or putting one's mouth to the earth in dust and ashes; eating or licking dust and ashes;—all these are common scriptural expressions for misery, helplessness, degradation, servitude, humiliation, and defeat. One may easily convince one's self of this, by consulting any full Concordance of the Bible. Let me cite a few notable instances; and in considering them, we should recall what is stated at pp. 14, 15, that in Hebrew the derivation itself of the word "belly" includes the idea of the bowing down and bending given in these texts, being from the same roots.

I.

Prostration, which, by bringing the belly to the earth and placing the mouth in the dust, as an analogous act with "going on the belly," is the ordinary Oriental and scriptural sign of subjection, of veneration, and of the acknowledgment of inferiority and submissive helplessness. I need hardly multiply cases. In Gen. xxxiii. 3, Jacob "bowed himself to the ground seven times, until he came near to his brother;"—xlii. 6, and xliii. 26, Joseph's brethren "bowed themselves to him to the earth;"—xliv. 14, "they fell before him upon the ground." Balaam, in Numb. xxii. 31, "bowed his head, and fell flat on his face." Ruth (ii. 10) "fell upon her face, and bowed herself to the ground." In 1 Sam. (Douay, 1 Kings) xx. 41, David in his distress "fell on his face to the ground, and bowed himself three times" to Jonathan;—xxv. 23, Abigail "fell before David on her face, and bowed herself to the ground;"—xxviii. 14, "Saul perceived that it was Samuel, and he stooped with his face to the ground, and bowed himself." In 2 Sam. (Douay, 2 Kings) i. 2, the messenger announcing Saul's death came, "with his clothes rent, and earth upon his head: and so it was, when he came to

David, that he fell to the earth, and did obeisance;"—xiv. 4, the woman of Tekoah "fell on her face to the ground, and did obeisance, and said, Help, O king;"—and ver. 22, "Joab fell to the ground on his face, and bowed himself;" and again, ver. 33, Absalom "came to the king, and bowed himself on his face to the ground before the king." In 1 Kings (Douay, 3 Kings) i. 23, Nathan "bowed himself before the king with his face to the ground." In 2 Kings (Douay, 4 Kings) ii. 15, the sons of the prophets "bowed themselves to the ground before" Elisha. In 1 Chron. xxi. 21, Ornan "bowed himself to David with his face to the ground." In 2 Chron. vii. 3, at the dedication of Solomon's temple, "when all the children of Israel saw how the fire came down, and the glory of the Lord upon the house, they bowed themselves with their faces to the ground upon the pavement, and worshipped, and praised the Lord."

Now, falling prostrate upon the ground, with the face to the earth, must necessarily bring the belly to the earth also. Thus this action, voluntary in the cases cited, corresponds to the involuntary compulsion, which was to be the punishment of Satan. Reluctantly, in spite of himself, and against his will, he would be compelled to give glory to

God, by being made prostrate, in helplessness, and by being forced to submit to His decrees.

II.

Next follows another group of phrases, which speak of dwelling, lying, or being in the dust; most of them being so worded as to include also the belly being upon the earth.

In Micah i. 9, 10, the prophet says of Samaria and Judah, "her wound is incurable . . . declare it not in Gath . . . in the house of dust roll thyself in the dust." In Nahum iii. 18, the prophet speaks of the downfall of Assyria—"thy nobles shall dwell in the dust."—Ps. vii. 6, "Let the enemy persecute my soul, and take it; yea, let him tread down my life upon the earth, and lay mine honour in the dust;"—xxii. (Douay, xxi.) 14, 15, "I am poured out like water, and all my bones are out of joint; my heart is like wax; it hath melted in the midst of my bowels; my strength is dried up like a potsherd; and my tongue cleaveth to my mouth; and Thou hast brought me to the dust of death;"—xliv. 24, 25, "Wherefore hidest Thou thy face, and forgettest our affliction and our oppression? For our soul is bowed down to the dust; our belly cleaveth to the earth," which is an evident equivalent to the phrase, "on thy belly shalt thou go;"—cxix. (Douay, cxviii.) 25, "My soul cleaveth unto the dust: quicken Thou me." Job (ii. 8), in his sore distress, "sat down among ashes;"—and ver. 13, his friends, sharing his affliction and misery, "sat down with him upon the ground seven days and seven nights;"—xvi. 15, "I have sewed sackcloth upon my skin, and defiled my horn in the dust;"—xxx. 19, "He hath cast me into the mire, and I am become like dust and ashes." Isa. iii. 25, 26, "And thy men shall fall by the sword, and thy mighty in the war; and her gates shall lament and mourn; and she being desolate shall sit upon the ground;"—xxvi. 19, "Awake ye and sing, ye that dwell in the dust;"—xxix. 4, speaking of the humiliation of Jerusalem, Isaiah prophesies, "And thou shalt be brought down, and thou shalt speak out of the ground; and thy speech shall be low out of the dust, and thy voice shall be as of one who hath a familiar spirit, out of the ground, and thy speech shall whisper out of the dust." Here we must note the well-known fact, that those who had familiar spirits, and those who were possessed, often fell in fits to the ground; and that similar epileptic fits often occurred at the delivery of pagan oracles. Isa. lii. 2, "Shake thyself from the dust; arise, sit down,

O Jerusalem; loose thyself from the bands of thy neck, O captive daughter of Zion." Jer. vi. 26, "O daughter of my people, gird thee with sackcloth, and wallow thyself in ashes: make thee mourning, as for an only son, most bitter lamentation;"—xxv. 33, "the slain of the Lord . . . shall not be lamented, neither gathered nor buried; they shall be as dung upon the ground;"—and ver. 34, "Howl, ye shepherds, and cry; wallow yourselves in ashes, ye principal of the flock; for the days of your slaughter and dispersion are accomplished, and ye shall fall." Lam. iii. 16, "He hath broken my teeth with gravel stones, He hath rolled me in the dust;"—and ver. 29, "He putteth his mouth in the dust, if so be that there may be hope."

III.

We have yet another group of passages, which speak of being cast down, or lying down, upon the ground, or dust, or earth, or ashes, or the dunghill;—always in the same sense of defeat, misery, and humiliation.

2 Sam. (Douay, 2 Kings) xii. 16, "David therefore besought God for the child; and David fasted, and went in, and lay all night upon the earth." Ps. cxlvii. (Douay, cxliv.) 9, "The Lord lifteth up the

meek; He casteth the wicked down to the ground." Isa. li. 22, 23, "Behold, I have taken out of thine hand the cup of trembling, even the dregs of the cup of My fury; thou shalt no more drink it again. But I will put it into the hand of them that afflict thee, which have said to thy soul, Bow down, that we may go over; and thou hast laid thy body as the ground, and as the street, to them that went over." Lam. ii. 10, "The elders of the daughter of Zion sit upon the ground, and keep silence: they have cast up dust upon their heads; they have girded themselves with sackcloth; the virgins of Jerusalem hang down their heads to the ground;"—and ver. 11, "Mine eyes fail with tears, my bowels are troubled, my liver is poured upon the earth, for the destruction of the daughter of my people" (the "liver" here being an equivalent for the "belly" in Gen. iii.);—iv. 5, "They that did feed delicately are desolate in the street; they that were brought up in scarlet embrace the dunghill." Ezek. xxvi. 16, "Then all the princes of the sea shall come down from their thrones, and lay away their robes, and put off their broidered garments; they shall clothe themselves with trembling; they shall sit down upon the ground, and shall tremble at every moment, and be astonished at thee;"—xxviii. 17,

"Thy heart was lifted up because of thy beauty, thou hast corrupted thy wisdom by reason of thy brightness; I will cast thee to the ground, I will lay thee before kings, that they may behold thee;" and ver. 18, "Thou hast defiled thy sanctuaries by the multitude of thine iniquities, by the iniquity of thy traffic; therefore will I bring forth a fire from the midst of thee, and it shall devour thee; and I will bring thee to ashes upon the earth, in the sight of all them that behold thee." Obad. 3, 4, "The pride of thine heart hath deceived thee, thou that dwellest in the clefts of the rocks, whose habitation is high; that saith in his heart, Who shall bring me down to the ground? Though thou exalt thyself as the eagle, and though thou set thy nest among the stars, thence will I bring thee down, saith the Lord."

IV.

We have yet one more and last group of phrases, which have a special reference to eating or licking dust or ashes.

Ps. lxxii. (Douay, lxxi.) 9, "They that dwell in the wilderness shall bow before Him; and His enemies shall lick the dust." Both these clauses are equivalent to the double clause of the curse on the Serpent; and here they actually again occur together, and in the same sense. Ps. cii. (Douay, ci.) 9, "For I have eaten ashes like bread, and mingled my drink with weeping; and ver. 10, "Because of Thine indignation and Thy wrath: for Thou hast lifted me up, and cast me down." This, too, has a close and evident parallel with Satan's former state, and his great fall and humiliation. Isa. xliv. 20, "He feedeth on ashes: a deceived heart hath turned him aside, that he cannot deliver his soul;" xlix. 23, "Kings shall be thy nursing fathers, and their queens thy nursing mothers: they shall bow down to thee with their face towards the earth, and lick up the dust of thy feet; and thou shalt know that I am the Lord." Here also we have the same two ideas of being cast to the ground and of eating dust, which occur in the curse on the Serpent, placed again in juxtaposition. Micah vii. 16, 17, "The nations shall see and shall be confounded at all their might: they shall lay their hands upon their mouth, their ears shall be deaf. They shall lick the dust like a serpent; they shall move out of their holes like worms of the earth: they shall be afraid of the Lord our God, and shall fear because of Thee." Here once again are the very same two ideas of the curse, in juxtaposition, though in inverted order. Again we have the creeping on the ground and the licking of dust placed side by side, as in Gen. iii.

In the last place I cite Isa. lxv., in which is a very striking passage indeed, having a direct reference to Gen. iii. It speaks of the punishment mentioned in Gen. iii., that the Serpent shall eat dust. It clearly states that this punishment had not yet taken effect in the prophet's days, but that it was still to be accomplished hereafter. He prophesies the calling of the Gentiles into the Church, and the rejection of the Jews for their incredulity and sins. Still, he says, a remnant shall be added to the number of the elect; the wicked shall be punished, and the godly rewarded. In the last place he describes the blessings and peace of the Church, or new Jerusalem; and, as the culminating point of these, he says (ver. 25), "The wolf and the lamb shall feed together, and the lion shall eat straw like the bullock: *and dust shall be the Serpent's meat.*"

In many of the foregoing texts a literal meaning is excluded by the very nature of the context. They are, however, phrases with a very clear and definite metaphorical meaning, which is, indeed, the same meaning as the words have in the natural and literal sense. They are all very clear proofs of what is the usage of Scriptural language in this matter. Prostration on the ground, dwelling or being on the ground, licking or eating dust and ashes,—all these are found to be cognate phrases, implying punishment, defeat, degradation, humiliation; voluntary or involuntary submission to a superior power; overthrow, and despair. With these expressions in our minds, we cannot fail to perceive plainly and distinctly the nature of the curse inflicted, in Gen. iii. 14, 15, on "the Serpent."

It may be paraphrased, as if God had thus spoken to "the Serpent," who is no other than Satan :—

For having caused the fall of man, and for opposing My will, "thou art cursed above all rational and irrational beings;" for they shall be able to fulfil their end, and to attain to the happiness of which their nature is capable. But thou shalt fail to be happy, having forfeited thy end; and thou shalt thus be more miserable and wretched than they. Immortal and spiritual as thou hast been, and art by nature, and must always be, thy punishment shall not be merely a temporary one, like that of Adam and Eve and their descendants.

They, if they choose, shall, after their short lives on this earth, still be able, through the grace of the Redemption which I shall presently announce, to rest for ever in heaven, and to enjoy an eternal happiness. Thy chance has been once for all forfeited without the possibility of any further hope. Thou hast exalted thyself against Me, in trying to ruin the work of My hands; I shall cast thee down and humble thee lower than thy victim; yea, and lower than "all the beasts of the field." I shall cast thee down to the earth; thou shalt grovel in the dust. Degraded from thy former high estate as thou art, thou shalt be yet further lowered and humbled. Every action thou dost shall add to thy condemnation and humiliation. Always thus grovelling on the earth, "on thy belly shalt thou go." Unable to rise, and powerless to exalt thyself, thou shalt feed on defeat, rage, and despair, and torture thyself with thy own feelings. "Dust shalt thou eat all the days of thy life."

This curse, therefore, is simply, in Scriptural language, a strong and clear expression for humiliation, defeat, rage, and despair. Satan was to be humbled most completely. His schemes were to be defeated, his power overthrown; and the ruin he had wrought was to be repaired by the Redeemer, promised in the next following verse.

The last-quoted text from Isaiah, moreover, proves that the curse was not considered by the prophet to have been accomplished immediately after it had been pronounced. It was not considered as quite accomplished even in the days of the prophet. This would not be the case had it referred to a bestial serpent, and to a corporeal going on its belly, to a material eating of dust. For all these should have been accomplished (in the commonly received theory) immediately after the condemnation. Yet the prophet still speaks of it in the future tense. It was, therefore, understood and proclaimed by the prophet as still awaiting accomplishment. It awaited its full, entire, and perfect realization till the time should come, not only for the death-blow to Satan's power by the death of our Lord Jesus Christ, but even for that further time, when the foreordained triumph of the Church, the spouse of the Lamb, was destined to put the final seal on the work of the redemption. Then, when all evil is exterminated, and eternal peace reigns, "dust shall be the Serpent's meat." For then shall be the complete triumph of God, and the complete overthrow and defeat of Satan.

This is to be the culminating climax of the Serpent's curse—his seeing the salvation of the human race on the last day.

In this sense the condemnation at once becomes intelligible, reasonable, and appropriate. No mere instrument is unnecessarily condemned. But the surpassing iniquity of "the Serpent," Satan, causes him, as he deserved, to be "cursed above all living beings"—both men and beasts—"on the earth." He is sentenced to eternal humiliation, defeat, and despair; cast flat to the earth, ever powerless to rise; feeding on what cannot sustain, nourish, or please; planning schemes destined beforehand to defeat; opposing when he knows and feels that he must always be conquered;—the abject, helpless, defeated enemy of Almighty Power and Infinite Goodness.

The next verse also (15,) of Gen. iii. assumes, in this interpretation, an appropriate meaning. "I will place enmity between thee and the woman, and between thy seed and her seed." It partly refers to the antagonism between Satan and mankind, whose eternal ruin in the individual he still ever continues to try to accomplish, as he then tried to do in its entire mass in the first pair. But the words are in the future tense: "I will put." They are, therefore, perfectly verified only in the antagonism between our blessed Saviour—the Seed of the woman, then promised as the future Avenger of man—and sin, the seed of "the Serpent," which our Lord came to destroy. Satan and sin—the Serpent and his seed—have warred, and still war, against the woman and her Seed; against the entire human race; against the plan of the redemption; against our Lord and His Church. This warfare will last till the end of time. In this war, the end will be that He shall crush the Serpent's head. Crushing a serpent's head means a complete victory over him; for it signifies death in the bestial, and utter overthrow in the Satanic, Serpent. That crushing will be completed in the day of general judgment. Then shall there be a complete and most unmistakable victory, manifested and declared in the united presence of God, the angels, the devils, and the entire human race. All shall see the wonderful working of the Providence of God. All shall see how His glory has been advanced by everything that had occurred on earth, even when Satan appeared for a time to conquer. "The Serpent's" design for the ruin of the human race shall be shown to have been completely overturned. His head shall be bruised in eternal death.

But in obtaining this victory, it was foretold that the conquered should, to a certain extent, injure the Conqueror: "Thou shalt bruise ['or attack'] His heel." Whether we consider the sufferings of our blessed Lord and all that the Redemption cost Him, or whether we look at the loss, notwithstanding that Redemption, of so many individual souls for whom He died, we see clearly verified both clauses of this portion of the curse of the Serpent.

If, therefore, to the admitted and glaring difficulties against the applicability of the clauses of this curse to the bestial serpent, we add the evident appropriateness of every clause in it under the interpretation which I have here ventured to give to it, we cannot surely fail to see in which direction the truth lies. Nor the less apparent and evident is the utter absence of any difficulty, and the complete disappearance of every improbability, from the narrative of the temptation and condemnation, when thus interpreted.

CHAPTER VIII.

ORIGIN OF THE COMMONLY RECEIVED INTERPRETATION.

AMONG the few points that still remain for explanation, the first is, How came the commonly received opinion to be so generally adopted in the Church, that Satan tempted Eve by means of a bestial serpent?

I venture to give what I trust will be found an easy and sufficient explanation.

The Church received the Old Testament from the Jewish synagogue. This narrative of Gen. iii. was not one of the controverted points between the old and the new dispensations. The early Christians read Gen. iii., and understood it, and taught it, and wrote upon it, in the sense in which it had been taught in the Jewish synagogue. That teaching, however, had long before ceased to be the mere literal teaching of what the sacred narrative really declared. There had gradually got mixed with it the eccentric and pretentious ideas of the Rabbis. The Talmud, the Mishna, and in general the writings of the Jewish Rabbis, are responsible for almost more absurdities than any other class of writings on earth. From them have proceeded many errors, and much defacement of the pure Judaism of the Holy Scriptures. One instance of their teachings may suffice, for it is to our point. One Rabbi teaches us (as Kircher relates) that, for the purpose of tempting Eve, a devil, whose name was Samael, came into Paradise riding on a camel, which was made in the shape of a serpent! After that, we need not be surprised that the generally received opinion was that Satan took possession of a bestial serpent to work out the fall of man.

From Judaism this teaching passed into the early Christian Church, as an unquestioned and undenied and uncriticized point of belief, though never an Article of Faith. Hence it continued to be taught in the same sense. There was then no criticism of passages of Scripture in the modern sense; no dissection of texts with reference to either philology or to rationalistic objections. The sole aim of commentators on this narrative was to explain a preconceived opinion—"*How* did the serpent tempt Eve?" And their explanation was what they had learned before, that Satan entered into a bestial serpent and used its organs for that purpose. It never struck them to inquire *who* was meant by "the Serpent." Not one of the difficulties which we have above detailed, entered for a moment in their minds. From their point of view no such difficulties could exist. They read the Holy Scriptures with a different object, and in a different manner, and with a different disposition, from those used at present. They were all engaged in making up an interpretation to suit a preconceived theory, and in answering, with more or less ingenuity, those objections against their theory which were then advanced. They were easily satisfied with the replies they wrote, and did not even take the trouble to verify what they stated as facts, on the authority of their predecessors. Not one of them seems to have tried to find out for himself the real sense of the sacred narrative according to its literal meaning. Not one seems to have investigated the meaning of obviously analogous phrases of Scripture. Some, conscious of difficulty, held it to be a myth, or figure, or allegory, and not an historical fact. But nearly all the others went on, in the name of the literal sense, to do violence to the literal sense of the sacred narrative, overloading it with gratuitous suppositions, and surrounding it with incorrect statements. They seem never to have considered the existence of that real scriptural Serpent—Satan—as a being quite distinct from the bestial serpent, and utterly unconnected with it. Much less did their readers or hearers.

But now arises the further question: Whence came the Rabbinical fable, introducing this supposed possession of a bestial serpent by Satan?

I think that we can trace it back to that intense fear and hatred of serpents which is, and has always been, prevalent in the East, owing to their being there so common and terrible a danger to human life. To Orientals, all serpents are an object of the intensest detestation; for in the East the deadly venom of the serpent is a standing menace, and a continual danger to man. Few, if any, innocuous serpents are there to be found; all are very formidable to man, with either poisonous bite or ponderous crushing coil. All creeping things, in fact, are an abomination to the Oriental mind. We have a significant proof in Lev. xi. 41, 42:
" And every creeping thing that creepeth upon the

earth shall be an abomination; it shall not be eaten. Whatsoever goeth upon the belly, and whatsoever goeth upon all four, or whatsoever hath more feet among all creeping things that creep upon the earth, them ye shall not eat; for they are an abomination." One would think that this was quite sufficient to mark the rejection of such animals for food. But no! With an emphasis altogether wanting in the rejection of other unclean animals, the sacred Lawgiver goes on, in vers. 43, 44: "Ye shall not make yourselves abominable with any creeping thing that creepeth, neither shall ye make yourselves unclean with them, that ye should be defiled thereby. For I am the Lord your God: ye shall therefore sanctify yourselves, and ye shall be holy; for I am holy: neither shall ye defile yourselves with any manner of creeping thing that creepeth upon the earth." Why this reiterated condemnation of creeping things as articles of food, with the extraordinary assertion of God's power and holiness, altogether omitted in other similar prohibitions? It may be said that the emphasis is due to this very supposition, that the serpent had been instrumental in the fall. But this cannot be. For the prohibition is not limited to those creeping things which go on the belly, but it is extended to all reptiles—even to those which, like lizards, crawl on four feet, and to those, like spiders and centipedes, which crawl on many feet. These are entirely different in form, nature, habit, and anatomy, from the serpent. They are not only specifically but generically distinct. The reason is simply a general reason; it is the antipathy of all Orientals, and of the sacred writer, Moses himself, to all creeping things. There is nothing more horrible, abominable, and detestable to the Oriental mind than creeping things; but among these the quick-gliding, silent, and deadly serpent is the climax of his hatred and terror. Moses (Exod. iv. 3) flies in terror when his rod is changed into a serpent, though immediately afterwards the appearance of even the loathly leprosy on his hand does not seem to disquiet him much. The forked tongue and deadly venom of the serpent (Ps. cxl. 3, and lviii. 4; Douay, cxxxix. and lvii.);—its uncertain and unascertainable course (Prov. xxx. 19);—its treacherous bite (Prov. xxiii. 32);—all exhibit the serpent as being to the Oriental mind the very type and symbol of whatever is most malignant, deceitful, and evil. The numerous and dreadful deaths in the desert from the bites of the fiery serpents (Numb. xxi. 6 and following verses) must have been quite fresh in the mind of the sacred writer of Gen. iii. That remembrance must have been perpetuated by the preservation of the brazen serpent, which had been very carefully kept, as is evident from 2 Kings (Douay, 4 Kings) xviii., etc. Those who have never been in the East, or have not lived in other countries where serpents are many and deadly, may think that I am exaggerating this terror and abomination, in order to prove my point. But it is quite the reverse. I have not said all that could be said. But, lest I be too prolix, I will add but one more proof. God, by the mouth of the Prophet Jeremiah (viii. 17), after mentioning numerous other punishments, including war and the devastation of their country, in punishment of the crimes of His people, holds out against them in the *last* place, and as the *most terrible* of all His punishments, a plague of serpents! " Behold, I will send serpents, cockatrices, among you, which shall not be charmed ; and they shall bite you, saith the Lord." How truly terrible to their minds must not that be, which is considered worse than even the horrors of war!

All this proves that to the Jews, as to other Orientals, there was nothing on earth worse, or more terrifying, or more antagonistic than the serpent. With such impressions in their minds and such feelings in their hearts, what wonder that they gave the name of "the Serpent"—to them the most odious and terrible of all things—to Satan, the arch-enemy of the human race, the subtil deceiver of Eve, the cause of all human ills! "He is an Arab to my sight," is the Turk's expression for any person he dislikes. Similarly Orientals express their detestation and horror of a thing by calling it a "serpent." Hence they gave to Satan (itself meaning "the Adversary") the name of "THE SERPENT." It was not because they originally believed that he had entered into, or used the bestial serpent, in any way while tempting Eve. It was because in his dealing with the human race, both in the case of Eve and ever afterwards, he had acted towards it as a deadly serpent might do with a human individual; creeping upon it unawares to deceive it; beguiling it with false and forked tongue; infecting its very nature with venomous poison; killing it with death-giving bite. For this reason Satan was justly abominable to man, and came by him to be called "the Serpent." For this same reason, also, the sacred writer of Gen. iii., wishing to represent Satan to his people as their worst enemy, called him "the Serpent"—to them the most terrible of all animals. For the same reason, further on in the curse, he uses words which still compare Satan to a serpent, making him metaphorically a "creeping thing," an object of utter abomination to his people. Most probably Satan had, long before the time of Moses, been commonly referred to under the name of "the Serpent." When Moses wrote of him by that title, he was doubtless clearly and distinctly understood by his people to mean Satan, and no bestial serpent. An expression well understood at one time, and under one set of circumstances might easily become ambiguous and doubtful under other circumstances of time, place, or persons. I may give here an instance of a somewhat similar phrase regarding serpents. In India, especially during the hours of darkness, the Hindoos will not speak of a serpent without an absolute necessity. But if they are compelled to speak of the animal at all, they will not call it by the usual names of *sanp* or *naga*. At such times they always speak of it as *russy*, a rope. Yet, when so spoken of, every one present clearly and at once understands the true meaning—when, for instance, one person out of a company inside a hut says that he "sees a rope in the garden." To a stranger, or under other circumstances, the expression might suggest a doubt of a literal meaning, and start him on the search for some figurative sense. But it is clear and intelligible enough to those to whom it is addressed.

So the sacred narrative, at the time that it was written, was doubtless perfectly intelligible to all for whom it was meant, that "the Serpent" meant Satan himself. Gradually it was allegorized. It began to be taken in various senses; much as some texts are used by preachers at all times in a very different sense from the original meaning. Then new and strange constructions began to be put upon it, and quaint stories built upon it, by the rabbinical writers and commentators, one of which I have already cited. In course of time the original meaning was overlaid with a fable, and the teaching settled down to the commonly received interpretation, that Satan had used a bestial serpent as his instrument in tempting Eve. This will furnish us with a very probable and sufficient origin for the common belief, till a better is found.

CHAPTER IX.

CONNECTION BETWEEN GEN. III. AND SERPENT-WORSHIP.

ANOTHER very important matter remains to be examined, and the difficulty it offers remains to be answered.

Numerous authors have been at very great pains to show that serpent-worship has been most widely diffused over the earth. They say that wherever there was idolatry, there was also serpent-worship. This would, of course, simply mean that it extended over the whole globe; for where has idolatry not prevailed at some time? They explain this universality of serpent-worship by the supposition that Satan, having ruined human nature by means of a serpent, and wishing to perpetuate that ruin by idolatry, kept alive the tradition that through the serpent came knowledge;

and thus induced men to worship him under that very form in which he had first effected man's ruin. Or the argument may be stated under a second form. The original tradition of the temptation and fall of man must be coextensive with the human race; and serpent-worship also is coextensive with the human race. This points to the truth of the belief that Eve must have been tempted by Satan under the form of a serpent; and that afterwards he so far succeeded in further seducing man, as to get himself worshipped universally under the form of a serpent, as the great benefactor of the human race, to which under that form he had communicated the godlike gifts of wisdom and of the knowledge of good and evil. Thus, for instance, argues Mr. Bathurst Deane, among others, in his learned and erudite work on "The Worship of the Serpent."

I may candidly admit that, if all that has been said and written of serpent-worship were strictly correct, this might prove an argument of some weight against the conclusion which I have endeavoured to establish. True serpent-worship, if universal, might perhaps, in some way, be used as a proof of a universal tradition of a temptation under the form of a serpent; whereas I have tried to prove that the temptation must have been effected directly, and without the aid of any serpent except Satan himself, spoken of under his scriptural title of "the Serpent."

In dealing with this matter, I shall examine it under three distinct heads: 1. What weight has it in determining that serpent-worship proves the theory of Satan's having used the bestial serpent as his instrument in tempting Eve? 2. Was serpent-worship really so universal as is represented? 3. What is the real origin and meaning of serpent-worship?

I shall discuss each point in a separate chapter.

CHAPTER X.

WHAT IS THE WEIGHT OF THE ARGUMENT FROM SERPENT-WORSHIP?

Two considerations will show us that the argument from serpent-worship is not a strong one in itself.

It would be a very strong one if there were no other hypothesis for the existence of serpent-worship than its supposed derivation from the incidents of the temptation of Eve. But, as I shall show in Chapter XII., the rise and progress of serpent-worship can be satisfactorily explained by a rival and better theory. Hence the mere fact (if it were a fact) that serpent-worship became prevalent, to a certain or to a great extent, throughout the world, would not of itself, prove the conclusion sought to be deduced from it. For if there is a second hypothesis, as good at least as the first, the conclusion would at best be a very doubtful one.

There is another point of great weakness in this hypothesis. If, as assumed, the serpent was known and acknowledged to have been the instrument of the fall of man, it would very naturally have become the object of detestation and abomination to man, rather than the object of his love and worship. It is easy to attribute this supposed, but most unnatural, result to the wiles of the arch-deceiver, Satan. I rather think he showed his wiliness in getting himself worshipped under indirect forms. No amount of wiliness could possibly make mankind, with such a tradition of the serpent alive among them, love and reverence and worship the very instrument of their ruin. To suppose the possibility of this, is to suppose a most irrational disposition in man.

Nor may it be said, in reply, that the serpent was worshipped as the cause of the knowledge of good and evil to man. For it is a very evident thing that Satan and the serpent could not be, and were not as a fact, either the cause or the occasion of the knowledge of good and evil. This knowledge of good and evil is essential to the nature of man, as a rational animal, endowed with an intellect and a will, and capable of knowing and serving God, his Creator. This knowledge must have been possessed by Adam and Eve at the very first instant of their creation; otherwise they could not have been real and perfect human beings. This knowledge must have existed in them, therefore, even before the suggestion of Satan, and before the eating of the forbidden fruit. If Adam and Eve had not already possessed this knowledge of discriminating between good and evil, they would have been utterly incapable of receiving a precept or command. It would have been quite useless for the Lord God to order them not to eat of any particular fruit; because, in the absence of knowledge, they could not have any free choice, which presupposes knowledge. Nor could they have incurred any responsibility in disobeying that command. Nor could they have committed any sinful act. Nor could they have deserved any punishment for their deed. All these things necessarily presuppose the knowledge of good and evil, which is essential to all rational beings. There cannot, therefore, be the slightest doubt that Adam and Eve, even in the first moment of their existence, possessed the use of intellect and free-will; and consequently the knowledge, together with the choice, of good and evil. These are essential to human nature.[1]

[1] It may be asked, What, then, are we to understand by the fact mentioned in Gen. ii. 9, that God planted in the garden of Eden "the tree of life, and the tree of the knowledge of good and evil"?

Whatever meaning we may seek to find in this passage, one thing is certain, namely, that it cannot mean that Adam and Eve did not know right from wrong, and good from evil, till they eat of the fruit of that particular tree. We readily admit that God could, by His almighty power, create a tree the fruit of which could have the power of conferring a knowledge of good and evil, where such knowledge did not naturally exist. But this was not at all necessary in the case of Adam and Eve, who naturally possessed that knowledge as part of their human nature. This is simply a plain and admitted point.

What is really meant by that tree being called "the tree of the knowledge of good and evil," is generally and rightly explained of experimental knowledge, which Adam and Eve acquired by sin—of their change from a good to an evil moral condition. I am inclined to add, that the word "knowledge" here may mean "test." There was no prohibition against the eating of the fruit of the tree of life. There was only one tree of which the fruit was forbidden (Gen. ii. 17 ; iii. 3). That was the one tree for causing a certain knowledge of good and evil. Not in Adam and Eve. Not that they did not already know good and evil. Not that the use of the fruit of that tree would confer on them that knowledge. Not that the knowledge would be acquired by Adam and Eve. But that it was *the test* by which God was to discriminate the good and obedient, from the evil or disobedient, among mankind. The knowledge which came from its use was no internal or subjective knowledge in the souls of those who eat of it; but it was the knowledge of them, that is to say, their *becoming known*, as good or bad, that it produced. It was not the agent, in an active sense, in producing knowledge in Adam and Eve. It was the means or occasion of a passive knowledge—that is, of the good being distinguished from the evil. It made known who were good and who were evil, serving the purpose of a test on the part of God.

This truth is so self-evident, that it is an insult to human nature to suppose that mankind could have ever been induced to believe universally that the serpent, by causing sin, communicated the knowledge of good and evil to man. The serpent, therefore, could never have been considered the cause or the occasion of the bestowal of reason upon man. Therefore, supposing the existence of such a tradition, namely, that the serpent was the instrument of the temptation and fall of man, it would naturally have been associated with the ideas of sin, evil, and ruin to man. It could not in any way have been looked upon as the bestower of reason. It is, therefore, utterly unnatural to suppose that it could ever, with such a tradition, have become the object of human worship. The tradition, therefore, fails to explain the origin of serpent-worship ; and, consequently, that tradition can receive no strength or support from serpent-worship, local or universal. This proof, therefore, fails signally, and is of but little weight.

But if this argument from the universality of serpent-worship is so weak and unnatural as I have just shown it to be, the very ground is cut away entirely from under it—such as it is—when we come to examine the next question.

CHAPTER XI.

WAS SERPENT-WORSHIP UNIVERSAL?

'Οφιολατρεία, or serpent-worship, is a study of such great extent, so vast in its literature and so varied in its details, that it would require a bold man to say that he had anything like a mastery of it. Nearly all the authors also who have written on the subject have tried to establish a connection between serpent-worship and the generally received opinion of the fall of man, through the instrumentality of a bestial serpent, and have declared and maintained that it was universal. Yet, with all due deference to them, I venture openly and boldly to contradict the universality of serpent-worship in itself. I do not speak diffidently on this matter, in spite of the learning and erudition, and the numbers of the authors who hold the opposite opinion. For I think that I have succeeded in detecting an important fallacy, pervading all their arguments and all the facts by which they support their assertions. It is not because of any overweening self-confidence, but because I feel that I should otherwise be wanting in the interests of truth, that I purpose here to show how very slight a consideration (as natural and necessary as it has simply been absolutely wanting) is sufficient to overturn the entire edifice of serpent-worship, with its superstructure of a supposed primæval tradition, in the commonly received sense.

Has serpent-worship really been universal or even almost universal?

All writers on serpent-worship say "Yes; it has." They go into minute details of all the countries where it was practised, and all the places where temples were erected for it. Assyria, Arabia, India, China, Palestine; Egypt, and all the rest of Africa; Greece and Rome; Scandinavia and Britain; North and South America, and many islands of the Pacific Ocean;—all these, that is to say, the whole world, are stated to have been given to serpent-worship. Anterior authors are cited; hundreds of facts are given; monuments are indicated, including temples, statues, rings, gems, obelisks, and tablets. All these are, with much labour, and ingenuity, and research, and erudition, marshalled to prove that serpent-worship was universal with the human race. But, the wish of being able to prove this having been the father to the thought, the usual results have followed. Statements have been accepted without examination. Suppositions have been largely dealt in, where proofs were wanting. Above all, a certain distinction has not been made, where it is most imperatively required. Even admitting all their facts and assertions and suppositions, this distinction, once made, is fatal to the assertion of the universality of serpent-worship. It is a simple distinction—one that they have all failed to use—and yet it is one which both can be and ought to be made.

All the writers whom I have been able to consult—and I have consulted a very great number—have confused two entirely different kinds of serpent-worship, which, if we are to arrive at the truth in the matter, must necessarily be carefully kept separate and examined apart.

Of these two things, one is serpent-worship, properly so called—the worship of the serpent as a god, *in himself* and *for his own sake*. This is *direct* serpent-worship. The other is serpent-worship, improperly so called; that is, the use and veneration of the serpent *not for himself*, but merely as the *symbol or emblem* of some one or more of the gods of different nations. This is *indirect* serpent-worship.[1]

The mere statement of this distinction will, I am certain, suffice to gain the assent of all my readers. That there is an essential difference between the two kinds, I think needs no proof. It is so self-evident as to have an irresistible claim on our minds as the voice of truth. It is these two entirely different kinds of serpent-worship which all authors on this subject confuse and blend into one, and treat of as one; as if there were no radical and essential difference between them. I take my stand by this distinction.

Now, even the most superficial glance at the works on serpent-worship will suffice to convince

[1] One very important fact may here be noted with reference to serpent-worship. In no country was it more prevalent than in Egypt. Yet among the objects of Egyptian worship was the *ibis*. And why? Because of its deadly hatred to serpents, which it instinctively sought out and killed! The serpent itself, therefore, could not have been the direct object of worship, for the Egyptians would not then have worshipped an animal for killing their god. The serpent, in itself, therefore was to them an object of fear and hatred, which they rejoiced to see killed. When they worshipped it, it was, and could only be, as the symbol of some other deity.

us, that nearly all that is there adduced regards serpent-worship *of the second kind*—that is, *indirect* serpent-worship—not for its own sake, but as a symbol of other gods. This is by no means true and real serpent-worship. It is, indeed, still a certain veneration of the serpent. But when that veneration is paid to it as the symbol of another, and solely for the sake of that other, and not for its own sake, then it is no longer directed to the serpent itself, but to that other. Therefore it is not really serpent-worship at all. Indirect serpent-worship can have no connection at all, not even an apparent one, with the history of the temptation as represented by the commonly received theory. All those facts of serpent-worship, therefore, which regard indirect serpent-worship as a symbol, are quite foreign to the question in hand. They have nothing to do with the temptation of Eve. They may and should, therefore, be quietly and simply put aside, as not being to the purpose.

Simple and necessary as this operation evidently is, it is surprising to see what terrible havoc and devastation it does to the fabric of serpent-worship. Down at one blow goes all that is piled up from the serpent-worship of China, India, Babylon,

Greece, Rome, Palestine, Arabia, Egypt, Scandinavia, Britain, and America; that is to say, the so-called serpent-worship of nearly the whole world!

All this was only indirect serpent-worship. In all these countries the serpent was simply the symbol or emblem of some god, with whom he had some either real or supposed connection. This god (and not the serpent) was the direct and sole object of the worship paid. It was a veneration extended to the serpent for the sake of this god—to one thing for the sake of another; not for its own sake, but simply and solely with reference to that other. It is like the veneration paid by Christians to the cross; not for the sake of the wood or image, but solely for the sake of Him who upon it, and by means of it, vouchsafed to redeem us from the slavery of sin. It is like the reverence and honour paid to a flag; not for the sake of its design or its material, but solely for the sake of the country of which it is the symbol.

After eliminating from the mass of what has been written regarding serpent-worship all those parts which treat of indirect serpent-worship as above described, we find very little indeed left for our consideration. The effect has been like that of sticking a knife into an inflated balloon. What remains is but as very little compared with what appeared before. And even in what little remains, we can still find place for a further reduction.

For, in examining even those cases in which we are told that living serpents were kept and fed in certain temples, and there venerated and worshipped, we shall still find that, even in these cases, —not many, after all—the great majority are still found to be nothing but instances of mere symbolic worship of the living serpent for its real or supposed connection with some god. The only difference is that in such cases a living and moving symbol was used instead of an engraved, carved, or sculptured one. The adoration is still indirect serpent-worship. In none of these cases, therefore, can it be said that real, direct serpent-worship, properly so called, existed. In other cases the serpent was kept, not as a real god or object of worship, but for the sake of being used as a means of taking auguries, by the method known to the ancients as ὀφιομαντεία, or divination by the serpent. In these cases no special sanctity would attach to the serpent, any more than to the flocks and herds bred for sacrificial purposes, or the birds employed by augurs.

Between these two objects for which living

serpents were used by the ancients, we fully cover nearly all the cases adduced of the veneration paid to the living animal, and (according to undiscriminating writers), for its living self.

I have refrained from quoting each particular case; both because it would swell these pages to an undesired extent, and because I am not *ex professo* engaged in combating these works on serpent-worship. But a very elementary knowledge of mythology will enable even the moderately educated to supply his own facts.

In each system of mythology the serpent is found to be the symbol of several gods. In Greece, for instance, he was the symbol of Apollo, of Minerva, of Juno, of Truth, etc. Yet everywhere he was but the symbol of a god. Nowhere is he the god himself—the direct object of worship. A mere worship of the symbol is not sufficient to constitute real serpent-worship. Real, direct serpent-worship, therefore, in its true sense, never was universally prevalent. It does not exist; it never existed universally. Symbolical serpent-worship did, but that does not help our opponents. The serpent itself, as such, never was worshipped, even generally, much less universally, as the superficial reader may have been led to believe, from the accounts furnished by writers, who have failed to make this fundamental distinction between direct and indirect serpent-worship.

But, even after eliminating all this mass of supposed serpent-worship, there still remain a few —very few—cases, adduced by professed writers on serpent-worship, of the adoration of the serpent for its own sake. These form the supposed cases of direct and properly so-called serpent-worship. These we are bound to examine briefly, and to explain.

1. There is the living serpent worshipped by the Ophites, a sect of ancient Gnostic heretics, which was kept, fed, and venerated in their temples, and which at their meetings was allowed, or rather invited, to wind amid the bread and wine of their Eucharist. But as they openly professed that this serpent was venerated as the symbol of our Lord, we may at once relegate this case to the class of symbolic adoration.

2. There is the history of Bel and the Dragon ("dragon" in Scripture simply meaning "a great serpent") narrated in the Book of Daniel, in a part which the Protestant Churches have relegated among the Apocryphal writings. But this dragon seems to have been only a living symbol of Bel

himself, for he had no separate temple or priests of his own, as each ancient god had. He was, it appears, kept in or near the temple of Bel; because, after the destruction of Bel, it is said, "And there was a great dragon in that place, and the Babylonians worshipped him" (ch. xv.). And he seems to have been ministered to by the priests of Bel; for it is said further on, "He hath destroyed Bel, he hath killed the dragon, and slain the priests"—mentioning only one set of priests for both. Daniel was not at first asked to worship this dragon or serpent, but to worship Bel. When Daniel objected to do so on the ground that Bel was only an inanimate object of brass and clay, and furthermore, when he had proved Bel's inability to do anything, even to eat, the king bethought him of the dragon. Turning then to Daniel, he said to him, that as this dragon was at least a living god, Daniel could not object to worshipping him. This, too, is therefore only another instance of veneration paid to a serpent, as the living symbol of a deity, as in the cases of Greek and Roman paganism.

3. The veneration of the Hindoos for living serpents is easily explained by their belief in the transmigration of souls, coupled on the one side

by their fear of the death-giving reptiles, and on the other with the fact that the serpent is, in their mythology, the symbol of *Shiva*, the Destroyer, the third god of their trinity, and the most powerful and dreaded of all their deities.

4. The only real cases of serpent-worship, direct and for its own sake, are found in a few tribes, among the most degraded, of Africa. This, however, is too small and insignificant a portion of the human race to adduce for so mighty a statement as the alleged universality of serpent-worship. Besides, even among these tribes, some substitute an iguana, or lizard, instead of the serpent. This shows us clearly that we must look for the origin of this local and degrading superstition in something very different from the ancient tradition of the fall of man, corrupted by human weakness.

There are literally no other *authenticated* cases of real direct serpent-worship to be met with even in the works of professed writers on this subject. And be it remembered that they are by no means particular or critical in the selection of their cases. As an instance of this, I give the following. Mr. Bathurst Deane, in his justly admired and learned work "The Worship of the Serpent," cites Bishop Pococke as furnishing us with an instance of real serpent-worship in modern Egypt; and he proceeds at once to adduce it in support of his theory—the commonly received one. Yet, on examining the case, what do we find? Simply a mass of contradiction, and supposition.

Pococke is told that in a certain place there dwells a holy serpent:—not so, said others; there are two of them. No one present had seen it, or could tell to which of the varieties of Egyptian serpents it belonged. It had been there, said some, from the time of Mohammed:—not at all, said others; it has been there since the day when the angel who accompanied Tobias bound Satan. All this might have convinced most men that this serpent was merely a legendary one. Not so Bishop Pococke. He goes to pay it a visit. He is taken to the place, and is told that the serpent dwells under the dome-covered mausoleum of a Mohammedan saint, in one of the clefts of the rock on which that mausoleum was built, while certain angels and devils and *jinns* dwelt in the neighbouring clefts. Most of us would have been fully convinced that the serpent was quite as mythical as the presence of those spirits. But not Bishop Pococke. He finds people bowing down and praying and kissing the ground, according to Mohammedan fashion, before a saint's tomb; and he concludes that they are worshipping this serpent. He sees signs of blood and entrails at the entrance of the mausoleum. The people, on being questioned, deny that sacrifices are offered to the serpent. Bishop Pococke forgets that Mohammedans, on certain feasts, sacrifice animals. In spite of everything, he jumps to the conclusion, that divine worship, in this case, really is paid to this living serpent which no one has seen, and which all deny to be a god! And Mr. Bathurst Deane adopts the tale!! I give this merely for the purpose of showing, by one instance, the uncriticizing and uncritical mode in which cases of so-called serpent-worship are related by travellers, honest doubtless in purpose, and otherwise men of learning and ability; and how they are blindly accepted by authors who have a theory to maintain, in aid of which they are ready to accept any asserted facts, no matter how inconsequential to their purpose, or how self-contradictory in their details.

Having thus set aside all direct worship of the serpent, except in a few cases in Africa, I shall speak briefly of the symbolical worship of the serpent.

The serpent was the symbol of various deities.

It represented among Greeks, the god of wisdom, of healing, of chastity, of agriculture, of war, of sensuality, of drunkenness. If, as asserted, serpent-worship was simply Satan-worship, under his favourite symbol of the animal by means of which he had achieved his greatest triumph, how came the serpent to represent agriculture (*Cybele*), chastity (*Pudicitia*), truth (*Veritas*), and healing (*Æsculapius*)? The arts of peace, the glories of self-mortification, the light of truth, the benefits of healing, are all diametrically opposed to what we know and can guess of the desires and wishes of Satan. The serpent could not, therefore, have been worshipped as the direct symbol of Satan himself. This also clearly proves that the serpent was regarded merely as a symbol of those deities; because he has not in himself any of the qualifications necessary to indicate those virtuous offices. He has not a multiplicity of attributes, powers, or influences, so as to have become the original object of worship, and to have been afterwards deified, under these various titles, into various gods. His worship began after he had been made the symbol. He is, therefore, simply a symbol, under various shapes and under diverse circumstances, of different gods, that had already been deified and worshipped for various reasons. Even when the serpent Python —representing Satan, or the Principle of Evil—is being slain by the Principle of Good, the serpent is shown as the symbol of the Good Principle, even during the actual destruction of the Evil Principle. A striking instance of this multifarious symbolic use of the serpent may be seen in the world-renowned statue known as the Belvedere Apollo.

> "Or view the lord of the unerring bow,
> The god of Life, of Poetry, and Light—
> The Sun in human form arrayed, and brow
> All radiant from his triumph in the fight;
> The shaft has just been shot—the arrow bright
> With an immortal's vengeance; in his eye
> And nostrils beautiful disdain, and might,
> And majesty flash their full lightnings by,
> Developing in that one glance the Deity."
>
> ("Childe Harold.")

It represents him, then, as having just discharged the bolt of death against Python. The handle of the bow is shown in his left hand, while the right arm and hand are thrown back in the attitude of an archer exulting in the accuracy of his aim. Yet, even while he is thus represented in the very act of triumphing over the Pythonic serpent, the Principle of Evil, there, to his right and behind him, coiled on the trunk of a tree, is again the serpent, the symbol of Apollo himself, the Good

Principle.[1] This multifarious use of the serpent for so many and such varied deities is a very strong proof that he is a mere symbol himself, and no deity.

[1] There is a cast of this statue in the Crystal Palace, in the same room as the models of the Forum, the Pantheon, and the Colosseum. The original, as all the world knows, is in the Vatican Museum in Rome.

CHAPTER XII.

ORIGIN OF SERPENT-WORSHIP.

IT is, of course, quite foreign to the purpose of this work to indicate an alternate hypothesis, different from that generally given, for the origin of the use of the serpent as a symbol of divinity, and for the consequent veneration of this symbol. Yet, lest I be accused of being one who can only rashly attack to destroy, and is impotent to build up, I may be allowed here briefly to sketch the skeleton of such an hypothesis. My limits will allow me to do no more.

God, the purest and simplest of all spiritual essences, has no shape or form of His own; and He could not, therefore, in the beginning, while the light of true tradition remained undimmed among men, be worshipped under any material image or representation. But in course of time, corrupt human nature hastened to represent the Deity to itself under sensible forms and images, chosen from the objects around them. At first these images and representations may have been used merely as symbols; but in course of time they became the objects themselves of idolatrous worship. Among such objects, the sun, the most impressive to man of all God's material works, and the most universally known, would certainly become the first, both in time and in rank, of all the subsequent objects of idolatry. The sun, as a matter of fact, is directly and in himself the chief god, or at least one of the chief gods, of every system of idolatry, absolutely all over the world. Wherever his enlightening beams penetrated and his vivifying influence was felt, there he was made a god, and became the direct object of real idolatrous worship. With the universal spread of this idolatry of the sun, came the necessity of adopting some object as a symbol to represent it, when its own form, or the human form of the sun-god, could not, for any special reason, be used. Such reasons might be the want of space, the maintenance of the secrets of mysteries, and others. Hence a symbol was adopted for the representation of this god, even as he had most probably been himself, in the beginning, the symbol of the one true and living God. That symbol was first found in the circle, because the sun is apparent to man always in that shape or form. In course of time the plain circle was improved upon, and was changed into the serpent-circle—that is to say, a serpent depicted in a circular form, with its tail in its mouth. Various reasons may be suggested for the adoption of the serpent, especially for the symbol of the sun.

1. Because of its apparent connection with the movements of the sun, with which it hybernates and grows torpid in winter, reappearing with renewed life and vigour when the sun returns northward with vernal heat rekindled.

2. Because each year, after winter, it renews its skin and apparent youth, as the sun seems to do each spring.

3. Because it loves to bask in the rays of the sun.

4. Because of its disc-like or circular shape when coiled up, which is its favourite position while at rest.

Whether these and other reasons are or are not the right ones, it is quite certain that in every country of the earth, and in every system of mythology, wherever sun-worship has prevailed—all over the world, in fact—the serpent is always the sure and inseparable symbol of the various sun-gods. There is, literally, no variety of mythological worship in which the serpent is not the chief symbol of the sun.

In process of time, the many qualities, real or supposed, of the sun came to be deified, each into a separate god. An analysis of mythology would prove this beyond a doubt. All these gods, however, having been but one in origin, continued to retain the original distinctive sun-symbol, the serpent. Once started on the downward path of idolatry, all nations went on adding gradually to the numbers of their gods. Then, by a communication of attributes, privileges, and qualities, all these gods, sharing in the idolatrous worship of the sun, came also to share with him the honour of having the serpent as their symbol. From this it followed that the serpent, become the symbol of numerous other deities, in time was adopted as the generic symbol of ALL divinity. Wherever a divinity was worshipped, the serpent, its symbol, was in constant use and veneration. Yet this veneration was given to it, not for itself, but merely as the symbol of the divinity. This, I am convinced, is one source of the origin and universality of the fact that the serpent has been chosen for veneration as the symbol and emblem of the divinity in every system of false worship.

There is yet a second source to point out. The greatest of all mysteries in the world is the existence and permission of evil. Its complete incomprehensibility led mankind very early into the dual worship of the Good and the Evil Principles. The Good Principle, however, was supposed, of His own nature, to be inclined to do good to all, and consequently to need no conciliation. On this account He was both less thought of and almost commonly forgotten, and His worship very generally neglected. On the contrary, the Evil Principle became the chief, almost the sole, object of the worship of the ignorant, owing to the fear which it caused in them, and owing to the belief that it was always meditating and contriving evil, and would certainly inflict it unless deprecated with worship and sacrifice. The serpent became the symbol of the Evil Principle, owing to his being a deadly terror to man in every country which was early peopled by the human race. The serpent's quick and silent course, its black, prominent, and unflinching eyes, its swift-darting and forked tongue, and, above all, its death-giving poisonous bite, constitute it a most malignant and terrible animal. Hence it was deemed the fittest to become the symbol of the Evil Principle. As the Evil Principle succeeded in drawing to itself all worship, to the almost utter exclusion of the Good Principle, it came, in course of time, to be looked upon as the principal, if not the sole divinity; and in consequence its symbol, the serpent, came to be regarded as the generic symbol of all divinity. Of this retirement of the worship of the Good before that of the Evil Principle, we have two clear proofs, among the many that might be adduced, in the deposition of Saturn, followed by the tripartite reign of Jupiter, Neptune, and Pluto; and in the absorbed self-contemplation of Bruhm, followed by the reign of the Hindoo trinity, Brahma, Vaishnu, and Shiva.

The serpent, originally the symbol of the Evil Principle, having in time become the generic symbol of all divinity, came to be used also as the symbol of the Good Principle whenever it became necessary to represent Him. Hence the well-known hieroglyph of the two serpents striving for the egg, that is—the Good and Evil Principles sharing the dominion of the earth.

These two sources of the origin of the symbol of the serpent for the Divinity, seem to account pretty satisfactorily for the universality, among the heathens, of symbolic or indirect serpent-worship.

Among the Jews, however, the author of all evil was not regarded as one of two equal gods. Their religion was a pure Monotheism. They were taught that the author of all evil was Satan, the chief of the angelic powers which rebelled against God. They found that the Principle of Evil all around them was symbolized by the serpent. Hence they also gave the name of "The Serpent" to Satan, the Principle, in their system, of all Evil. Thus this rebel angel-chief came to be indiscriminately called Satan and "the Serpent," and was equally well understood and known under both titles, by the Jews.

Summary of Serpent-worship.

I may now briefly sum up the results obtained in this discussion on serpent-worship. We have drawn the following conclusions:—

1. Real serpent-worship, directly paid to the serpent for its own sake, is too limited and local to merit any special attention; and as it occurs

precisely among the most degraded specimens of the human race, we conclude that it is not a relic preserved from the deposit of ancient, pure, and primæval tradition, but merely a case of local human degeneration.

2. Even the very few cases of apparently direct serpent-worship given by writers on this subject, are found, on closer examination, to be easily resolved into cases of symbolic worship, as above.

3. In all other cases serpent-worship is found to be merely an indirect veneration of the serpent, as the symbol, emblem, sign, or representation of some other god, notably the sun; which god, and not the serpent itself, is the real object of worship.

4. In course of time the serpent was adopted as the generic symbol of all divinity, and was used as the emblem of both the Good and the Evil Principle, but more specially and frequently of the latter. Hence among the Jews it became both the emblem and the name of Satan.

5. The asserted universality of serpent-worship, therefore, is not a fact. The statements made (*bonâ fide*, no doubt, but still without objective truth) are due solely to the uncritical want of distinguishing between real and symbolic serpent-worship. This distinction is both essential in itself,

and necessary for the full understanding of the matter.

6. Not being universal—in fact, not being even common—no argument can be drawn from so-called serpent-worship to prove that it indicates any ancient and universal tradition of Satan's having seduced Eve by means of a serpent.

7. The details and facts, therefore, of serpent-worship, so laboriously, laudably, and usefully collected by writers like Mr. Bathurst Deane, Bryant, and Faber, cannot be said to oppose what I am trying to maintain, namely, that no material serpent was used by Satan in tempting Eve.

8. Lastly, we have obtained a clear and substantial indication of the manner in which Satan came, not only to be called "the Serpent" by Moses, in Gen. iii., but also commonly, both before and after his time.

CHAPTER XIII.

CONCLUSION.

It will be a useful thing to conclude with a brief summary of what has been shown in these pages.

We have seen that the interpretation of Gen. iii. presents serious difficulties, which render untenable the explanation commonly received; and that the other theories are absolutely undeserving of serious consideration. The objections against the use, in any way, of a bestial serpent by Satan or its acting of itself, are many.

1. The serpent is by no means the most subtil of all living beings.

2. It could not naturally talk; and Satan's talking through it would have ensured the defeat of his scheme, by exciting Eve's suspicions.

3. It is not cursed above all animals.

4. Going on its belly is to the bestial serpent

no curse, but only its natural mode of progression.

5. It does not and cannot feed on dust.

6. There is no special enmity between it and man, above other animals.

7. God's justice would not allow Him to curse the innocent and irrational instrument of Satan's malice.

8. The Redeemer did not, in any sense, crush the head of any bestial serpent.

9. No particular bestial serpent could have lived till the coming of "the Seed."

10. The serpent is not said to have come or gone, either at the time and place of the temptation, or at the time and place of the condemnation. Yet the presence of a bestial serpent, under the circumstances, would not have been tolerated by Adam and Eve, even in their hiding-place.

11. As the text speaks of one special serpent, there is no rational explanation which of the many was the tempter, and how it became superior to its mates.

12. Making this one serpent to be different in wisdom and nature from the others, contradicts the Scripture, that all animals, male and female, were created "in their kind."

13. If by "the Serpent" is meant the bestial instrument of Satan, then Satan himself, the real tempter as all admit, is nowhere at all mentioned in the sacred narrative.

14. One serpent alone, as the sole cause of the evil, is cursed. Hence, if it were a bestial one, it must have lived, till its death, differently from other serpents, which would be anomalous. Or they must have shared its curse, without having had any, even material, part in the evil. This would be unjust and absurd.

15. This serpent is represented as acting of his own natural powers, for there is no statement of a superior being in it. These powers, however, of the bestial serpent are incompatible with such acts as are related in Gen. iii.

16. It is not stated to have been possessed, or guided, or aided, or used by any one else, for a purpose that was not its own. That Satan used a bestial serpent is, therefore, a purely gratuitous assertion, unfounded in the narrative. The text speaks of ONE BEING only as tempting, that is " the Serpent," and not of TWO, Satan *and* the serpent.

17. The literal sense of the sacred narrative is violated by introducing Satan as possessing the serpent and using it for his purpose.

18. Satan, the author of all this evil, would thus escape all condemnation; for only three are cursed—Adam, Eve, and this one serpent.

19. The Prophet Isaiah represents the curse as still remaining to be accomplished, and that only at the end of the world.

20. If going on its belly and eating dust were verified in the bestial serpent that tempted Eve, and the crushing of the head in the Satanic Serpent, Satan, then there follows the absurdity of one curse being directed partly against one and partly against the other, without any sign being furnished by the sacred writer as to the change thus made.

21. Moreover, the first part of the same curse would be taken in a literal sense, and the second part—the bruising—in a metaphorical sense. Now, two such senses are absolutely inadmissible in one and the same sentence.

22. There is no possible metaphorical sense in which the bestial serpent could "eat dust."

23. No bestial serpent that we know bruised our blessed Lord's heel, or injured Him in any way, as it was foretold that the Serpent of Gen. iii. should do.

24. No reason has ever been given why this one

particular bestial serpent is called, *par excellence*, "the Serpent," as he expressly is in the Hebrew text.

These objections seem to render untenable all theories involving any part taken by a bestial serpent in the temptation. This failure authorizes us to seek for any further explanation that we may be able to draw, from the words of the Holy Scriptures themselves. The necessity for that search justifies us in quitting the assumed *communem sententiam* of Fathers and commentators, as has been done in some similar cases, with advantage.

In the very beginning of such a search, we find, on careful consideration of the Hebrew text, that our translations are by no means strictly accurate, though they are, to all intents and purposes, sufficiently correct. We find that the accurate meaning would run precisely thus: "A certain Serpent was more intelligent than all the living beings of the earth that the Lord God had made. . . Cursed art thou above all beasts and above all living beings on the earth."

We find that these words are absolutely inapplicable to the bestial serpent, in any reasonable sense. We find, on further examination of the Holy Scriptures, that there is a certain Serpent repeatedly mentioned in them, which is quite distinct from the bestial serpent, and which ranks among the chief works of God, and which formerly held a very high and exalted position in the universe. We find, moreover, that this Serpent is expressly called "The Serpent, he of old;" and that he is to eat dust at the end of the world. He is thus clearly designated as the same being who is mentioned in Gen. iii. We learn, moreover, that he is expressly mentioned as the same being who under one name is called "the Serpent;" and under other names is called "the Dragon," "the Devil," and "Satan." We therefore conclude that by the words, "the Serpent," in Gen. iii., the sacred writer meant no bestial or apparitional serpent, either working of itself or working under external and superior agency; but that he there meant this same Serpent, Satan, acting in his own person and individuality. We find that, only one Tempter being mentioned, and that one, as shown, being Satan, called "The Serpent,"—there is no room left for supposing the presence or act of any other serpent, bestial or apparitional.

On further continuing our examination of the sacred narrative of Gen. iii., and comparing it with parallel passages of Holy Scripture, we find that in the narrative Satan, "the Serpent," fits in as appropriately and naturally, as the bestial serpent had been completely out of place and impossible. We conclude, therefore, that in Gen. iii. "the Serpent" is literally a name of Satan, to the exclusion of any other serpent, as he is himself a real serpent, nay, *par excellence*, "the Serpent."

Many reasons urge us to hold that "the Serpent" means Satan alone and by himself.

1. Satan was, it is admitted by all, the real agent in the temptation. Yet, throughout Gen. iii., he is neither mentioned nor hinted at, unless it be done under the title of "the Serpent." Either, therefore, Satan did nothing; or he did everything, and then he alone is himself "the Serpent."

2. Satan, "the Serpent," certainly is (as the bestial serpent is not) the most subtil among all living beings on the earth; for he had been once a leader among even the greatest angels, and he has not lost his natural faculties and powers by his fall.

3. A startling preternatural phenomenon, like the talking of a bestial serpent with a human voice, would have been no proof of subtility, but just the reverse; for it would have been calculated, of its very nature, to defeat the purpose which "the Serpent" had in view.

4. On the other hand, a very serious and real temptation, unaccompanied with any preternatural circumstances, could be caused by the Serpent, Satan ; for, by the spiritual intercommunication of thoughts, he could cause thoughts and desires to arise in Eve under the appearance of being the spontaneous acts of her own soul. This would indeed be a very master-stroke of subtility. That this is what really took place is suggested by the interjection, "Strange ! that God hath said."

5. The omission of all mention of the coming and going of the serpent, which has already been thrice dwelt upon, is perfectly right and appropriate, when we hold that the sacred narrative is speaking of an incorporeal and spiritual being. It coincides perfectly with the nature and doings of Satan, who, we are told, "as a roaring lion walketh about, seeking whom he may devour" (1 Pet. v. 8), though always invisible and inaudible.

6. After the curse, "the Serpent" is not again mentioned, though the sacred narrative proceeds to describe how the curse operated on the other two. Adam and Eve's expulsion from Eden is expressly mentioned ; as also are the facts that Adam tilled the ground, and Eve brought forth children. The working of their curses—material

punishments—is recorded, because they began at once. The Serpent's curse is not related as having begun. Another Scripture tells us that its operation was not to be completed for ages to come. This confirms the impression that it was a spiritual, and not a material, curse. Hence Gen. iii. does not describe it as even beginning to operate.

7. Each clause of the curse on "the Serpent," which makes absolute nonsense in the supposition of a bestial serpent, is appropriately verified, in a definite scriptural sense, in the supposition of Satan being "the Serpent."

8. If Satan was not himself "the Serpent," then he alone, of all those concerned in the fall, would escape without any punishment whatsoever, although he was really the most guilty of all, and, in fact, the prime mover and cause of all the evil.

9. Satan did, and no other then living serpent could, continue to live till "the Seed of the woman" came, in the Person of our Lord Jesus Christ, to crush his head; that is to say, to repair the effects of the fall.

10. With the substitution of Satan as "the Serpent," all those difficulties, which unquestionably attend the sacred narrative in Gen. iii., vanish

at once, and it becomes perfectly intelligible and reasonable.

11. This interpretation makes no gratuitous suppositions, on which all others are manifestly grounded.

12. Satan is expressly called "the Serpent" in several passages of Holy Scripture, and in many of them with special allusions to Gen. iii.

13. This is, therefore, a perfectly literal, nay, the only really literal, interpretation of Gen. iii., without suppositions, allegories, myths, metaphors, or impossibilities.

14. Satan's head was bruised by the death of our Lord; and Satan did metaphorically bruise His heel, in His Passion. These two clauses cannot, in any possible sense, be made applicable to a bestial serpent.

I have, moreover, considered the sacred narrative in its supposed connection with serpent-worship; and I have, I trust, proved that no argument can be drawn from serpent-worship against the interpretation which I have advocated, or in favour of the past theories. I have also tried to furnish a satisfactory and sufficient reason why Satan came to be called "The Serpent" by Moses.

Having now reached the end of my task, I have

but a few more words to add. I have tried not to be unduly severe or harsh in criticizing other theories and interpretations. I have tried to give a clear view of each; to state succinctly the difficulties in its way, to put fully what is advanced in its defence, and to state plainly what I considered its defects. I have ventured to advance another theory and interpretation, taking my key from Rev. (Apocalypse) xii. I wished to show that this interpretation is the only strictly literal one; that it makes no gratuitous suppositions, unfounded in Holy Writ; that it fits perfectly and naturally into the sacred narrative; that it appropriately suits every clause of the text; that it obviates all the difficulties attending the other interpretations; that it has the usage of Scripture in its favour; and that it presents the sacred narrative before us, not only as a possible occurrence, but it also furnishes a probable, natural, consistent, appropriate, and rational explanation of the manner in which "the Serpent"—Satan—tempted Eve, and was punished for his crime. This is what I wished to do; it is for others to judge with what success I have tried.

APPENDIX.

Genesis III., according to the Hebrew Text.

1. וְהַנָּחָשׁ הָיָה עָרוּם מִכֹּל חַיַּת הַשָּׂדֶה
The-Serpent was intelligent among-all living-(beings) of-the-field

אֲשֶׁר עָשָׂה יְהוָֹה אֱלֹהִים וַיֹּאמֶר אֶל־הָאִשָּׁה אַף
which had-made the-Lord God. And-he-said to-the-woman: Strange!

כִּי־אָמַר אֱלֹהִים לֹא תֹאכְלוּ מִכֹּל עֵץ הַגָּן׃
that-has-said God not shall-ye-eat of-every-tree of-the-garden!

2. וַתֹּאמֶר הָאִשָּׁה אֶל־הַנָּחָשׁ מִפְּרִי עֵץ־הַגָּן
And-said the-woman to-the-Serpent, Of-the-fruit of-(each)-tree-of-the-garden

נֹאכֵל׃
we-may-eat.

3. וּמִפְּרִי הָעֵץ אֲשֶׁר בְּתוֹךְ־הַגָּן אָמַר
But-of-the-fruit of-the-tree which (is)-in-the-midst-of-the-garden, hath-said

אֱלֹהִים לֹא תֹאכְלוּ מִמֶּנּוּ וְלֹא תִגְּעוּ בּוֹ פֶּן־תְּמֻתוּן׃
God not shall-ye-eat of-it and-not shall-ye-touch it, lest-perhaps-ye-die.

4. וַיֹּאמֶר הַנָּחָשׁ אֶל־הָאִשָּׁה לֹא־מוֹת תְּמֻתוּן:
And-said the-Serpent, to-the-woman, Not-dying shall-ye-die.

5. כִּי יוֹדֵעַ אֱלֹהִים כִּי בְּיוֹם אֲכָלְכֶם מִמֶּנּוּ וְנִפְקְחוּ
For knoweth God that in-the-day ye-eat of-it, will-be-opened

עֵינֵיכֶם וִהְיִיתֶם כֵּאלֹהִים יֹדְעֵי טוֹב וָרָע:
your-eyes, and-ye-shall-be as-gods, knowing good and-evil.

. . . .

13. . . . וַתֹּאמֶר הָאִשָּׁה הַנָּחָשׁ הִשִּׁיאַנִי וָאֹכֵל:
And-said the-woman, The-Serpent deceived-me, and-I-did-eat.

14. וַיֹּאמֶר יְהֹוָה אֱלֹהִים אֶל־הַנָּחָשׁ כִּי עָשִׂיתָ זֹּאת
And-said the-Lord God to-the-Serpent, Because thou-hast-done this,

אָרוּר אַתָּה מִכָּל־הַבְּהֵמָה וּמִכֹּל חַיַּת הַשָּׂדֶה
cursed (art) thou above-every-beast and-every living-(being) of-the-field.

עַל־גְּחֹנְךָ תֵלֵךְ וְעָפָר תֹּאכַל כָּל־יְמֵי חַיֶּיךָ:
Upon-thy-belly shalt-thou-go, and-dust shalt-thou-eat, all-the-days of-thy-life.

15. וְאֵיבָה אָשִׁית בֵּינְךָ וּבֵין הָאִשָּׁה
And-enmity I-will-put between-thee and-between the-woman;

וּבֵין זַרְעֲךָ וּבֵין זַרְעָהּ הוּא יְשׁוּפְךָ רֹאשׁ
and-between thy-seed and-between her-seed. He shall-crush thy-head,

וְאַתָּה תְּשׁוּפֶנּוּ עָקֵב:
and-thou shalt-crush his-heel.

Genesis III., from the Greek Septuagint
(Tischendorf's Edition of the Codex Vaticanus).

1. Ὁ δὲ ὄφις ἦν φρονιμώτατος πάντων τῶν θηρίων ἐπὶ τῆς γῆς ὧν ἐποίησε ὁ Θεός. Καὶ εἶπεν ὁ ὄφις τῇ γυναικὶ, Τί ὅτι εἶπεν ὁ Θεός, Οὐ μὴ φάγητε ἀπὸ παντὸς ξύλου τοῦ παραδείσου;

2. Καὶ εἶπεν ἡ γυνὴ τῷ ὄφει, Ἀπὸ καρποῦ τοῦ ξύλου τοῦ παραδείσου φαγούμεθα·

3. Ἀπὸ δὲ τοῦ καρποῦ τοῦ ξύλου ὅ ἐστιν ἐν μέσῳ τοῦ παραδείσου, εἶπεν ὁ Θεός, Οὐ φάγεσθε ἀπ' αὐτοῦ οὐ δὲ μὴ ἅψησθε αὐτοῦ, ἵνα μὴ ἀποθάνητε.

4. Καὶ εἶπεν ὁ ὄφις τῇ γυναικὶ, Οὐ θανάτῳ ἀποθανεῖσθε·

5. Ἤδει γὰρ ὁ Θεὸς ὅτι ᾗν ἂν ἡμέρᾳ φάγητε ἀπ' αὐτοῦ διανοιχθήσονται ὑμῶν οἱ ὀφθαλμοὶ, καὶ ἔσεσθε ὡς θεοί, γινώσκοντες καλὸν καὶ πονηρόν.

6. Καὶ εἶδεν ἡ γυνὴ ὅτι καλὸν τὸ ξύλον εἰς βρῶσιν, καὶ ὅτι ἀρεστὸν τοῖς ὀφθαλμοῖς ἰδεῖν, καὶ ὡραῖόν ἐστι τοῦ κατανοῆσαι, καὶ λαβοῦσα ἀπὸ τοῦ καρποῦ αὐτοῦ ἔφαγε· καὶ ἐδώκε καὶ τῷ ἀνδρί αὐτῆς μετ' αὐτῆς, καὶ ἔφαγον.

. . . . . .

13. Καὶ εἶπε Κύριος ὁ Θεὸς τῇ γυναικὶ, Τί τοῦτο ἐποίησας; καὶ εἶπεν ἡ γυνὴ, Ὁ ὄφις ἠπάτησέ με, καὶ ἔφαγον.

14. Καὶ εἶπεν Κύριος ὁ Θεὸς τῷ ὄφει, Ὅτι ἐποίησας τοῦτο, ἐπικατάρατος σὺ ἀπὸ πάντων τῶν κτηνῶν καὶ ἀπὸ παντῶν τῶν θηρίων ἐπὶ τῆς γῆς· ἐπὶ τῷ στήθει σοῦ καὶ τῇ κοιλίᾳ πορεύσῃ, καὶ γῆν φαγῇ πάσας τάς ἡμέρας τῆς ζωῆς σοῦ.

15. Καὶ ἔχθραν θήσω ἀνὰ μέσον σοῦ καὶ ἀνὰ μέσον τῆς γυναικὸς, καὶ ἀνὰ μέσον τοῦ σπέρματὸς σοῦ καὶ ἀνὰ μέσον τοῦ σπέρματος αὐτῆς. Αὐτός σοῦ τηρήσει κεφαλήν, καὶ σὺ τηρήσεις αὐτοῦ πτέρναν.

APPROBATION OF SUPERIORS.

Nihil obstat.
  J. B., Canonicus Cahill,
    Censor Deputatus.

Imprimatur,
  ✝ JOANNES, *Ep. Portmouthensis.*

Imprimatur,
  ✝ EDUARDUS, *Ep. Nottinghamiensis*

PRINTED BY WILLIAM CLOWES AND SONS, LIMITED,
LONDON AND BECCLES.

A LIST OF
KEGAN PAUL, TRENCH & CO.'S PUBLICATIONS.

11.87.

1, *Paternoster Square,*
London.

A LIST OF
KEGAN PAUL, TRENCH & CO.'S
PUBLICATIONS.

CONTENTS.

	PAGE		PAGE
GENERAL LITERATURE.	2	MILITARY WORKS.	33
PARCHMENT LIBRARY	18	POETRY.	35
PULPIT COMMENTARY	21	NOVELS AND TALES	41
INTERNATIONAL SCIENTIFIC SERIES	30	BOOKS FOR THE YOUNG	43

GENERAL LITERATURE.

A. K. H. B.—From a Quiet Place. A Volume of Sermons. Crown 8vo, 5s.

ALEXANDER, *William, D.D., Bishop of Derry.*—The Great Question, and other Sermons. Crown 8vo, 6s.

ALLIES, *T. W., M.A.*—Per Crucem ad Lucem. The Result of a Life. 2 vols. Demy 8vo, 25s.

　A Life's Decision. Crown 8vo, 7s. 6d.

AMHERST, *Rev. W. J.*—The History of Catholic Emancipation and the Progress of the Catholic Church in the British Isles (chiefly in England) from 1771-1820. 2 vols. Demy 8vo, 24s.

AMOS, *Professor Sheldon.*—The History and Principles of the Civil Law of Rome. An aid to the Study of Scientific and Comparative Jurisprudence. Demy 8vo, 16s.

Ancient and Modern Britons. A Retrospect. 2 vols. Demy 8vo, 24s.

ARISTOTLE.—The Nicomachean Ethics of Aristotle. Translated by F. H. Peters, M.A. Third Edition. Crown 8vo, 6s.

AUBERTIN, *J. J.*—A Flight to Mexico. With 7 full-page Illustrations and a Railway Map of Mexico. Crown 8vo, 7s. 6d.

AUBERTIN, J. J.—continued.
> Six Months in Cape Colony and Natal. With Illustrations and Map. Crown 8vo, 6s.

Aucassin and Nicolette. Edited in Old French and rendered in Modern English by F. W. BOURDILLON. Fcap 8vo, 7s. 6d.

AUCHMUTY, A. C.—Dives and Pauper, and other Sermons. Crown 8vo, 3s. 6d.

AZARIUS, Brother.—Aristotle and the Christian Church. Small crown 8vo, 3s. 6d.

BADGER, George Percy, D.C.L.—An English-Arabic Lexicon. In which the equivalent for English Words and Idiomatic Sentences are rendered into literary and colloquial Arabic. Royal 4to, 80s.

BAGEHOT, Walter.—The English Constitution. Fourth Edition. Crown 8vo, 7s. 6d.

> Lombard Street. A Description of the Money Market. Eighth Edition. Crown 8vo, 7s. 6d.

> Essays on Parliamentary Reform. Crown 8vo, 5s.

> Some Articles on the Depreciation of Silver, and Topics connected with it. Demy 8vo, 5s.

BAGOT, Alan, C.E.—Accidents in Mines: their Causes and Prevention. Crown 8vo, 6s.

> The Principles of Colliery Ventilation. Second Edition, greatly enlarged. Crown 8vo, 5s.

> The Principles of Civil Engineering as applied to Agriculture and Estate Management. Crown 8vo, 7s. 6d.

BAIRD, Henry M.—The Huguenots and Henry of Navarre. 2 vols. With Maps. 8vo, 24s.

BALDWIN, Capt. J. H.—The Large and Small Game of Bengal and the North-Western Provinces of India. With 20 Illustrations. New and Cheaper Edition. Small 4to, 10s. 6d.

BALL, John, F.R.S.—Notes of a Naturalist in South America. With Map. Crown 8vo, 8s. 6d.

BALLIN, Ada S. and F. L.—A Hebrew Grammar. With Exercises selected from the Bible. Crown 8vo, 7s. 6d.

BARCLAY, Edgar.—Mountain Life in Algeria. With numerous Illustrations by Photogravure. Crown 4to, 16s.

BASU, K. P., M.A.—Students' Mathematical Companion. Containing problems in Arithmetic, Algebra, Geometry, and Mensuration, for Students of the Indian Universities. Crown 8vo, 6s.

BAUR, *Ferdinand, Dr. Ph.*—A Philological Introduction to Greek and Latin for Students. Translated and adapted from the German, by C. KEGAN PAUL, M.A., and E. D. STONE, M.A. Third Edition. Crown 8vo, 6s.

BAYLY, *Capt. George.*—Sea Life Sixty Years Ago. A Record of Adventures which led up to the Discovery of the Relics of the long-missing Expedition commanded by the Comte de la Perouse. Crown 8vo, 3s. 6d.

BENSON, *A. C.*—William Laud, sometime Archbishop of Canterbury. A Study. With Portrait. Crown 8vo, 6s.

BIRD, *Charles, F.G.S.*—Higher Education in Germany and England. Small crown 8vo, 2s. 6d.

Birth and Growth of Religion. A Book for Workers. Crown 8vo, cloth, 2s.; paper covers, 1s.

BLACKBURN, *Mrs. Hugh.*—Bible Beasts and Birds. 22 Illustrations of Scripture photographed from the Original. 4to, 42s.

BLECKLY, *Henry.*—Socrates and the Athenians: An Apology. Crown 8vo, 2s. 6d.

BLOOMFIELD, *The Lady.*—Reminiscences of Court and Diplomatic Life. New and Cheaper Edition. With Frontispiece. Crown 8vo, 6s.

BLUNT, *The Ven. Archdeacon.*—The Divine Patriot, and other Sermons. Preached in Scarborough and in Cannes. New and Cheaper Edition. Crown 8vo, 4s. 6d.

BLUNT, *Wilfrid S.*—The Future of Islam. Crown 8vo, 6s.

Ideas about India. Crown 8vo. Cloth, 6s.

BODDY, *Alexander A.*—To Kairwân the Holy. Scenes in Muhammedan Africa. With Route Map, and Eight Illustrations by A. F. JACASSEY. Crown 8vo, 6s.

BOSANQUET, *Bernard.*—Knowledge and Reality. A Criticism of Mr. F. H. Bradley's "Principles of Logic." Crown 8vo, 9s.

BOUVERIE-PUSEY, *S. E. B.*—Permanence and Evolution. An Inquiry into the Supposed Mutability of Animal Types. Crown 8vo, 5s.

BOWEN, *H. C., M.A.*—Studies in English. For the use of Modern Schools. Ninth Thousand. Small crown 8vo, 1s. 6d.

English Grammar for Beginners. Fcap. 8vo, 1s.

Simple English Poems. English Literature for Junior Classes. In four parts. Parts I., II., and III., 6d. each. Part IV., 1s. Complete, 3s.

BRADLEY, *F. H.*—The Principles of Logic. Demy 8vo, 16s.

BRIDGETT, *Rev. T. E.*—History of the Holy Eucharist in Great Britain. 2 vols. Demy 8vo, 18s.

BROOKE, *Rev. Stopford A.*—**The Fight of Faith.** Sermons preached on various occasions. Fifth Edition. Crown 8vo, 7s. 6d.

The Spirit of the Christian Life. Third Edition. Crown 8vo, 5s.

Theology in the English Poets.—Cowper, Coleridge, Wordsworth, and Burns. Sixth Edition. Post 8vo, 5s.

Christ in Modern Life. Sixteenth Edition. Crown 8vo, 5s.

Sermons. First Series. Thirteenth Edition. Crown 8vo, 5s.

Sermons. Second Series. Sixth Edition. Crown 8vo, 5s.

BROWN, *Horatio F.*—**Life on the Lagoons.** With 2 Illustrations and Map. Crown 8vo, 6s.

Venetian Studies. Crown 8vo, 7s. 6d.

BROWN, *Rev. J. Baldwin.*—**The Higher Life.** Its Reality, Experience, and Destiny. Sixth Edition. Crown 8vo, 5s.

Doctrine of Annihilation in the Light of the Gospel of Love. Five Discourses. Fourth Edition. Crown 8vo, 2s. 6d.

The Christian Policy of Life. A Book for Young Men of Business. Third Edition. Crown 8vo, 3s. 6d.

BURDETT, *Henry C.*—**Help in Sickness—Where to Go and What to Do.** Crown 8vo, 1s. 6d.

Helps to Health. The Habitation—The Nursery—The Schoolroom and—The Person. With a Chapter on Pleasure and Health Resorts. Crown 8vo, 1s. 6d.

BURKE, *Oliver J.*—**South Isles of Aran (County Galway).** Crown 8vo, 2s. 6d.

BURKE, *The Late Very Rev. T. N.*—**His Life.** By W. J. FITZPATRICK. 2 vols. With Portrait. Demy 8vo, 30s.

BURTON, *Lady.*—**The Inner Life of Syria, Palestine, and the Holy Land.** Post 8vo, 6s.

CANDLER, *C.*—**The Prevention of Consumption.** A Mode of Prevention founded on a New Theory of the Nature of the Tubercle-Bacillus. Demy 8vo, 10s. 6d.

CAPES, *J. M.*—**The Church of the Apostles:** an Historical Inquiry. Demy 8vo, 9s.

Carlyle and the Open Secret of His Life. By HENRY LARKIN. Demy 8vo, 14s.

CARPENTER, *W. B., LL.D., M.D., F.R.S., etc.*—**The Principles of Mental Physiology.** With their Applications to the Training and Discipline of the Mind, and the Study of its Morbid Conditions. Illustrated. Sixth Edition. 8vo, 12s.

Catholic Dictionary. Containing some Account of the Doctrine, Discipline, Rites, Ceremonies, Councils, and Religious Orders of the Catholic Church. By WILLIAM E. ADDIS and THOMAS ARNOLD, M.A. Third Edition. Demy 8vo, 21*s*.

Century Guild Hobby Horse. Vol. I. Half parchment, 12*s*. 6*d*.

CHARLES, *Rev. R. H.*—**Forgiveness, and other Sermons.** Crown 8vo, 4*s*. 6*d*.

CHEYNE, *Canon.*—**The Prophecies of Isaiah.** Translated with Critical Notes and Dissertations. 2 vols. Fourth Edition. Demy 8vo, 25*s*.

    Job and Solomon; or, the Wisdom of the Old Testament. Demy 8vo, 12*s*. 6*d*.

    The Psalter; or, The Book of the Praises of Israel. Translated with Commentary. Demy 8vo.

CLAIRAUT.—**Elements of Geometry.** Translated by Dr. KAINES. With 145 Figures. Crown 8vo, 4*s*. 6*d*.

CLAPPERTON, *Jane Hume.*—**Scientific Meliorism and the Evolution of Happiness.** Large crown 8vo, 8*s*. 6*d*.

CLARKE, *Rev. Henry James, A.K.C.*—**The Fundamental Science.** Demy 8vo, 10*s*. 6*d*.

CLODD, *Edward, F.R.A.S.*—**The Childhood of the World**: a Simple Account of Man in Early Times. Eighth Edition. Crown 8vo, 3*s*.

    A Special Edition for Schools. 1*s*.

    The Childhood of Religions. Including a Simple Account of the Birth and Growth of Myths and Legends. Eighth Thousand. Crown 8vo, 5*s*.

    A Special Edition for Schools. 1*s*. 6*d*.

    Jesus of Nazareth. With a brief sketch of Jewish History to the Time of His Birth. Small crown 8vo, 6*s*.

COGHLAN, *J. Cole, D.D.*—**The Modern Pharisee and other Sermons.** Edited by the Very Rev. H. H. DICKINSON, D.D., Dean of Chapel Royal, Dublin. New and Cheaper Edition. Crown 8vo, 7*s*. 6*d*.

COLERIDGE, *Sara.*—**Memoir and Letters of Sara Coleridge.** Edited by her Daughter. With Index. Cheap Edition. With Portrait. 7*s*. 6*d*.

COLERIDGE, *The Hon. Stephen.*—**Demetrius.** Crown 8vo, 5*s*.

CONNELL, *A. K.*—**Discontent and Danger in India.** Small crown 8vo, 3*s*. 6*d*.

    The Economic Revolution of India. Crown 8vo, 4*s*. 6*d*.

COOK, *Keningale, LL.D.*—**The Fathers of Jesus.** A Study of the Lineage of the Christian Doctrine and Traditions. 2 vols. Demy 8vo, 28*s*.

CORR, *the late Rev. T. J., M.A.*—**Favilla**; Tales, Essays, and Poems. Crown 8vo, 5s.

CORY, *William.*—**A Guide to Modern English History.** Part I.—MDCCCXV.-MDCCCXXX. Demy 8vo, 9s. Part II.—MDCCCXXX.-MDCCCXXXV., 15s.

COTTON, *H. J. S.*—**New India, or India in Transition.** Third Edition. Crown 8vo, 4s. 6d.; Cheap Edition, paper covers, 1s.

COUTTS, *Francis Burdett Money.*—**The Training of the Instinct of Love.** With a Preface by the Rev. EDWARD THRING, M.A. Small crown 8vo, 2s. 6d.

COX, *Rev. Sir George W., M.A., Bart.*—**The Mythology of the Aryan Nations.** New Edition. Demy 8vo, 16s.

Tales of Ancient Greece. New Edition. Small crown 8vo, 6s.

A Manual of Mythology in the form of Question and Answer. New Edition. Fcap. 8vo, 3s.

An Introduction to the Science of Comparative Mythology and Folk-Lore. Second Edition. Crown 8vo, 7s. 6d.

COX, *Rev. Sir G. W., M.A., Bart.,* and *JONES, Eustace Hinton.*—**Popular Romances of the Middle Ages.** Third Edition, in 1 vol. Crown 8vo, 6s.

COX, *Rev. Samuel, D.D.*—**A Commentary on the Book of Job.** With a Translation. Second Edition. Demy 8vo, 15s.

Salvator Mundi; or, 'Is Christ the Saviour of all Men? Tenth Edition. Crown 8vo, 5s.

The Larger Hope. A Sequel to "Salvator Mundi." Second Edition. 16mo, 1s.

The Genesis of Evil, and other Sermons, mainly expository. Third Edition. Crown 8vo, 6s.

Balaam. An Exposition and a Study. Crown 8vo, 5s.

Miracles. An Argument and a Challenge. Crown 8vo, 2s. 6d.

CRAVEN, *Mrs.*—**A Year's Meditations.** Crown 8vo, 6s.

CRAWFURD, *Oswald.*—**Portugal, Old and New.** With Illustrations and Maps. New and Cheaper Edition. Crown 8vo, 6s.

CRUISE, *Francis Richard, M.D.*—**Thomas à Kempis.** Notes of a Visit to the Scenes in which his Life was spent. With Portraits and Illustrations. Demy 8vo, 12s.

CUNNINGHAM, *W., B.D*—**Politics and Economics:** An Essay on the Nature of the Principles of Political Economy, together with a survey of Recent Legislation. Crown 8vo, 5s.

DANIELL, *Clarmont.*—**The Gold Treasure of India.** An Inquiry into its Amount, the Cause of its Accumulation, and the Proper Means of using it as Money. Crown 8vo, 5s.

DANIELL, *Clarmont.—continued.*
>Discarded Silver: a Plan for its Use as Money. Small crown 8vo, 2s.

DANIEL, *Gerard.* Mary Stuart: a Sketch and a Defence. Crown 8vo, 5s.

DARMESTETER, *Arsene.*—The Life of Words as the Symbols of Ideas. Crown 8vo, 4s. 6d.

DAVIDSON, *Rev. Samuel, D.D., LL.D.*—Canon of the Bible: Its Formation, History, and Fluctuations. Third and Revised Edition. Small crown 8vo, 5s.

>The Doctrine of Last Things contained in the New Testament compared with the Notions of the Jews and the Statements of Church Creeds. Small crown 8vo, 3s. 6d.

DAWSON, *Geo., M.A.* Prayers, with a Discourse on Prayer. Edited by his Wife. First Series. Ninth Edition. Crown 8vo, 3s. 6d.

>Prayers, with a Discourse on Prayer. Edited by GEORGE ST. CLAIR. Second Series. Crown 8vo, 6s.

>Sermons on Disputed Points and Special Occasions. Edited by his Wife. Fourth Edition. Crown 8vo, 6s.

>Sermons on Daily Life and Duty. Edited by his Wife. Fourth Edition. Crown 8vo, 6s.

>The Authentic Gospel, and other Sermons. Edited by GEORGE ST. CLAIR, F.G.S. Third Edition. Crown 8vo, 6s.

>Biographical Lectures. Edited by GEORGE ST. CLAIR, F.G.S. Third Edition. Large crown 8vo, 7s. 6d.

>Shakespeare, and other Lectures. Edited by GEORGE ST. CLAIR, F.G.S. Large crown 8vo, 7s. 6d.

DE JONCOURT, *Madame Marie.*—Wholesome Cookery. Fourth Edition. Crown 8vo, cloth, 1s. 6d; paper covers, 1s.

DENT, *H. C.*—A Year in Brazil. With Notes on Religion, Meteorology, Natural History, etc. Maps and Illustrations. Demy 8vo, 18s.

Doctor Faust. The Old German Puppet Play, turned into English, with Introduction, etc., by T. C. H. HEDDERWICK. Large post 8vo, 7s. 6d.

DOWDEN, *Edward, LL.D.*—Shakspere: a Critical Study of his Mind and Art. Eighth Edition. Post 8vo, 12s.

>. Studies in Literature, 1789–1877. Fourth Edition. Large post 8vo, 6s.

>Transcripts and Studies. Large post 8vo.

Dulce Domum. Fcap. 8vo, 5s.

DU MONCEL, *Count.*—The Telephone, the Microphone, and the Phonograph. With 74 Illustrations. Third Edition. Small crown 8vo, 5*s.*

DUNN, *H. Percy.*—Infant Health. The Physiology and Hygiene of Early Life. Crown 8vo.

DURUY, *Victor.*—History of Rome and the Roman People. Edited by Prof. MAHAFFY. With nearly 3000 Illustrations. 4to. 6 vols. in 12 parts, 30*s.* each vol.

Education Library. Edited by Sir PHILIP MAGNUS:—

    An Introduction to the History of Educational Theories. By OSCAR BROWNING, M.A. Second Edition. 3*s.* 6*d.*

    Old Greek Education. By the Rev. Prof. MAHAFFY, M.A. Second Edition. 3*s.* 6*d.*

    School Management. Including a general view of the work of Education, Organization and Discipline. By JOSEPH LANDON. Sixth Edition. 6*s.*

EDWARDES, *Major-General Sir Herbert B.*—Memorials of his Life and Letters. By his Wife. With Portrait and Illustrations. 2 vols. Demy 8vo, 36*s.*

ELSDALE, *Henry.*—Studies in Tennyson's Idylls. Crown 8vo, 5*s.*

Emerson's (Ralph Waldo) Life. By OLIVER WENDELL HOLMES. English Copyright Edition. With Portrait. Crown 8vo, 6*s.*

"Fan Kwae" at Canton before Treaty Days 1825-1844. By an old Resident. With Frontispiece. Crown 8vo, 5*s.*

Five o'clock Tea. Containing Receipts for Cakes, Savoury Sandwiches, etc. Fcap. 8vo, cloth, 1*s.* 6*d.*; paper covers, 1*s.*

FOTHERINGHAM, *James.*—Studies in the Poetry of Robert Browning. Crown 8vo. 6*s.*

GARDINER, *Samuel R.,* and *J. BASS MULLINGER, M.A.*—Introduction to the Study of English History. Second Edition. Large crown 8vo, 9*s.*

Genesis in Advance of Present Science. A Critical Investigation of Chapters I.-IX. By a Septuagenarian Beneficed Presbyter. Demy 8vo, 10*s.* 6*d.*

GEORGE, *Henry.*—Progress and Poverty: An Inquiry into the Causes of Industrial Depressions, and of Increase of Want with Increase of Wealth. The Remedy. Fifth Library Edition. Post 8vo, 7*s.* 6*d.* Cabinet Edition. Crown 8vo, 2*s.* 6*d.* Also a Cheap Edition. Limp cloth, 1*s.* 6*d.*; paper covers, 1*s.*

    Protection, or Free Trade. An Examination of the Tariff Question, with especial regard to the Interests of Labour. Second Edition. Crown 8vo, 5*s.*

GEORGE, *Henry.—continued.*
> Social Problems. Fourth Thousand. Crown 8vo, 5s. Cheap Edition, paper covers, 1s.

GILBERT, *Mrs.*—Autobiography, and other Memorials. Edited by Josiah Gilbert. Fifth Edition. Crown 8vo, 7s. 6d.

GLANVILL, *Joseph.*—Scepsis Scientifica; or, Confest Ignorance, the Way to Science; in an Essay of the Vanity of Dogmatizing and Confident Opinion. Edited, with Introductory Essay, by John Owen. Elzevir 8vo, printed on hand-made paper, 6s.

Glossary of Terms and Phrases. Edited by the Rev. H. Percy Smith and others. Second and Cheaper Edition. Medium 8vo, 7s. 6d.

GLOVER, *F., M.A.*—Exempla Latina. A First Construing Book, with Short Notes, Lexicon, and an Introduction to the Analysis of Sentences. Second Edition. Fcap. 8vo, 2s.

GOODENOUGH, *Commodore J. G.*—Memoir of, with Extracts from his Letters and Journals. Edited by his Widow. With Steel Engraved Portrait. Third Edition. Crown 8vo, 5s.

GORDON, *Major-General C. G.*—His Journals at Kartoum. Printed from the original MS. With Introduction and Notes by A. Egmont Hake. Portrait, 2 Maps, and 30 Illustrations. Two vols., demy 8vo, 21s. Also a Cheap Edition in 1 vol., 6s.
> Gordon's (General) Last Journal. A Facsimile of the last Journal received in England from General Gordon. Reproduced by Photo-lithography. Imperial 4to, £3 3s.
> Events in his Life. From the Day of his Birth to the Day of his Death. By Sir H. W. Gordon. With Maps and Illustrations. Second Edition. Demy 8vo, 7s. 6d.

GOSSE, *Edmund.*—Seventeenth Century Studies. A Contribution to the History of English Poetry. Demy 8vo, 10s. 6d.

GOULD, *Rev. S. Baring, M.A.*—Germany, Present and Past. New and Cheaper Edition. Large crown 8vo, 7s. 6d.
> The Vicar of Morwenstow. A Life of Robert Stephen Hawker. Crown 8vo, 6s.

GOWAN, *Major Walter E.*—A. Ivanoff's Russian Grammar. (16th Edition.) Translated, enlarged, and arranged for use of Students of the Russian Language. Demy 8vo, 6s.

GOWER, *Lord Ronald.* My Reminiscences. Miniature Edition, printed on hand-made paper, limp parchment antique, 10s. 6d.
> Bric-à-Brac. Being some Photoprints taken at Gower Lodge, Windsor. Super royal 8vo.
> Last Days of Mary Antoinette. An Historical Sketch. With Portrait and Facsimiles. Fcap. 4to, 10s. 6d.

GOWER, *Lord Ronald.—continued.*

    Notes of a Tour from Brindisi to Yokohama, 1883-1884. Fcap. 8vo, 2s. 6d.

GRAHAM, *William, M.A.*—The Creed of Science, Religious, Moral, and Social. Second Edition, Revised. Crown 8vo, 6s.

    The Social Problem, in its Economic, Moral, and Political Aspects. Demy 8vo, 14s.

GREY, *Rowland.*—In Sunny Switzerland. A Tale of Six Weeks. Second Edition. Small crown 8vo, 5s.

    Lindenblumen and other Stories. Small crown 8vo, 5s.

GRIMLEY, *Rev. H. N., M.A.*—Tremadoc Sermons, chiefly on the Spiritual Body, the Unseen World, and the Divine Humanity. Fourth Edition. Crown 8vo, 6s.

    The Temple of Humanity, and other Sermons. Crown 8vo, 6s.

GURNEY, *Edmund.*—Tertium Quid : chapters on Various Disputed Questions. 2 vols. Crown 8vo, 12s.

HADDON, *Caroline.*—The Larger Life, Studies in Hinton's Ethics. Crown 8vo, 5s.

HAECKEL, *Prof. Ernst.*—The History of Creation. Translation revised by Professor E. RAY LANKESTER, M.A., F.R.S. With Coloured Plates and Genealogical Trees of the various groups of both Plants and Animals. 2 vols. Third Edition. Post 8vo, 32s.

    The History of the Evolution of Man. With numerous Illustrations. 2 vols. Post 8vo, 32s.

    A Visit to Ceylon. Post 8vo, 7s. 6d.

    Freedom in Science and Teaching. With a Prefatory Note by T. H. HUXLEY, F.R.S. Crown 8vo, 5s.

Hamilton, Memoirs of Arthur, B.A., of Trinity College, Cambridge. Crown 8vo, 6s.

Handbook of Home Rule, being Articles on the Irish Question by Various Writers. Edited by JAMES BRYCE, M.P. Second Edition. Crown 8vo, 1s. sewed, or 1s. 6d. cloth.

HARRIS, *William.*—The History of the Radical Party in Parliament. Demy 8vo, 15s.

HAWEIS, *Rev. H. R., M.A.*—Current Coin. Materialism—The Devil—Crime—Drunkenness—Pauperism—Emotion—Recreation—The Sabbath. Fifth Edition. Crown 8vo, 5s.

    Arrows in the Air. Fifth Edition. Crown 8vo, 5s.

    Speech in Season. Fifth Edition. Crown 8vo, 5s.

    Thoughts for the Times. Fourteenth Edition. Crown 8vo, 5s.

HAWEIS, Rev. H. R., M.A.—continued.

    Unsectarian Family Prayers. New Edition. Fcap. 8vo, 1s. 6d.

HAWTHORNE, Nathaniel.—**Works.** Complete in Twelve Volumes. Large post 8vo, 7s. 6d. each volume.

HEATH, Francis George.—**Autumnal Leaves.** Third and cheaper Edition. Large crown 8vo, 6s.

    Sylvan Winter. With 70 Illustrations. Large crown 8vo, 14s.

Hegel's Philosophy of Fine Art. The Introduction, translated by BERNARD BOSANQUET. Crown 8vo, 5s.

HENNESSY, Sir John Pope.—**Ralegh in Ireland.** With his Letters on Irish Affairs and some Contemporary Documents. Large crown 8vo, printed on hand-made paper, parchment, 10s. 6d.

HENRY, Philip.—**Diaries and Letters of.** Edited by MATTHEW HENRY LEE, M.A. Large crown 8vo, 7s. 6d.

HINTON, J.—**Life and Letters.** With an Introduction by Sir W. W. GULL, Bart., and Portrait engraved on Steel by C. H. Jeens. Fifth Edition. Crown 8vo, 8s. 6d.

    Philosophy and Religion. Selections from the Manuscripts of the late James Hinton. Edited by CAROLINE HADDON. Second Edition. Crown 8vo, 5s.

    The Law Breaker, and The Coming of the Law. Edited by MARGARET HINTON. Crown 8vo, 6s.

    The Mystery of Pain. New Edition. Fcap. 8vo, 1s.

Homer's Iliad. Greek text, with a Translation by J. G. CORDERY. 2 vols. Demy 8vo, 24s.

HOOPER, Mary.—**Little Dinners: How to Serve them with Elegance and Economy.** Twentieth Edition. Crown 8vo, 2s. 6d.

    Cookery for Invalids, Persons of Delicate Digestion, and Children. Fifth Edition. Crown 8vo, 2s. 6d.

    Every-Day Meals. Being Economical and Wholesome Recipes for Breakfast, Luncheon, and Supper. Seventh Edition. Crown 8vo, 2s. 6d.

HOPKINS, Ellice.—**Work amongst Working Men.** Sixth Edition. Crown 8vo, 3s. 6d.

HORNADAY, W. T.—**Two Years in a Jungle.** With Illustrations. Demy 8vo, 21s.

HOSPITALIER, E.—**The Modern Applications of Electricity.** Translated and Enlarged by JULIUS MAIER, Ph.D. 2 vols. Second Edition, Revised, with many additions and numerous Illustrations. Demy 8vo, 25s.

HOWARD, Robert, M.A.—The Church of England and other Religious Communions. A course of Lectures delivered in the Parish Church of Clapham. Crown 8vo, 7s. 6d.

How to Make a Saint; or, The Process of Canonization in the Church of England. By the PRIG. Fcap 8vo, 3s. 6d.

HUNTER, William C.—Bits of Old China. Small crown 8vo, 6s.

HYNDMAN, H. M.—The Historical Basis of Socialism in England. Large crown 8vo, 8s. 6d.

IDDESLEIGH, Earl of.—The Pleasures, Dangers, and Uses of Desultory Reading. Fcap. 8vo, in Whatman paper cover, 1s.

IM THURN, Everard F.—Among the Indians of Guiana. Being Sketches, chiefly anthropologic, from the Interior of British Guiana. With 53 Illustrations and a Map. Demy 8vo, 18s.

JACCOUD, Prof. S.—The Curability and Treatment of Pulmonary Phthisis. Translated and edited by MONTAGU LUBBOCK, M.D. Demy 8vo, 15s.

Jaunt in a Junk: A Ten Days' Cruise in Indian Seas. Large crown 8vo, 7s. 6d.

JENKINS, E., and RAYMOND, J.—The Architect's Legal Handbook. Third Edition, revised. Crown 8vo, 6s.

JENKINS, Rev. Canon R. C.—Heraldry: English and Foreign. With a Dictionary of Heraldic Terms and 156 Illustrations. Small crown 8vo, 3s. 6d.

The Story of the Caraffa; the Pontificate of Paul IV. Small crown 8vo, 3s. 6d.

JOEL, L.—A Consul's Manual and Shipowner's and Shipmaster's Practical Guide in their Transactions Abroad. With Definitions of Nautical, Mercantile, and Legal Terms; a Glossary of Mercantile Terms in English, French, German, Italian, and Spanish; Tables of the Money, Weights, and Measures of the Principal Commercial Nations and their Equivalents in British Standards; and Forms of Consular and Notarial Acts. Demy 8vo, 12s.

JOHNSTON, H. H., F.Z.S.—The Kilima-njaro Expedition. A Record of Scientific Exploration in Eastern Equatorial Africa, and a General Description of the Natural History, Languages, and Commerce of the Kilima-njaro District. With 6 Maps, and over 80 Illustrations by the Author. Demy 8vo, 21s.

JORDAN, Furneaux, F.R.C.S.—Anatomy and Physiology in Character. Crown 8vo, 5s.

JOYCE, P. W., LL.D., &c.—Old Celtic Romances. Translated from the Gaelic. Crown 8vo, 7s. 6d.

KAUFMANN, *Rev. M., B.A.*—**Socialism : its Nature, its Dangers, and its Remedies** considered. Crown 8vo, 7s. 6d.

Utopias ; or, Schemes of Social Improvement, from Sir Thomas More to Karl Marx. Crown 8vo, 5s.

KAY, *David, F.R.G.S.*—**Education and Educators.** Crown 8vo. 7s. 6d.

KAY, *Joseph.*—**Free Trade in Land.** Edited by his Widow. With Preface by the Right Hon. JOHN BRIGHT, M.P. Seventh Edition. Crown 8vo, 5s.

*** Also a cheaper edition, without the Appendix, but with a Review of Recent Changes in the Land Laws of England, by the RIGHT HON. G. OSBORNE MORGAN, Q.C., M.P. Cloth, 1s. 6d. ; paper covers, 1s.

KELKE, *W. H. H.*—**An Epitome of English Grammar for the Use of Students.** Adapted to the London Matriculation Course and Similar Examinations. Crown 8vo, 4s. 6d.

KEMPIS, *Thomas à.*—**Of the Imitation of Christ.** Parchment Library Edition.—Parchment or cloth, 6s. ; vellum, 7s. 6d. The Red Line Edition, fcap. 8vo, cloth extra, 2s. 6d. The Cabinet Edition, small 8vo, cloth limp, 1s. ; cloth boards, 1s. 6d. The Miniature Edition, cloth limp, 32mo, 1s.

*** All the above Editions may be had in various extra bindings.

Notes of a Visit to the Scenes in which his Life was spent. With numerous Illustrations. By F. R. CRUISE, M.D. Demy 8vo, 12s.

KETTLEWELL, *Rev. S.*—**Thomas à Kempis and the Brothers of Common Life.** With Portrait. Second Edition. Crown 8vo, 7s. 6d.

KIDD, *Joseph, M.D.*—**The Laws of Therapeutics ;** or, the Science and Art of Medicine. Second Edition. Crown 8vo, 6s.

KINGSFORD, *Anna, M.D.*—**The Perfect Way in Diet.** A Treatise advocating a Return to the Natural and Ancient Food of our Race. Third Edition. Small crown 8vo, 2s.

KINGSLEY, *Charles, M.A.*—**Letters and Memories of his Life.** Edited by his Wife. With two Steel Engraved Portraits, and Vignettes on Wood. Sixteenth Cabinet Edition. 2 vols. Crown 8vo, 12s.

*** Also a People's Edition, in one volume. With Portrait. Crown 8vo, 6s.

All Saints' Day, and other Sermons. Edited by the Rev. W. HARRISON. Third Edition. Crown 8vo, 7s. 6d.

True Words for Brave Men. A Book for Soldiers' and Sailors' Libraries. Sixteenth Thousand. Crown 8vo, 2s. 6d.

KNOX, *Alexander A.*—**The New Playground ;** or, Wanderings in Algeria. New and Cheaper Edition. Large crown 8vo, 6s.

Kosmos; or, the Hope of the World. 3*s*. 6*d*.

Land Concentration and Irresponsibility of Political Power, as causing the Anomaly of a Widespread State of Want by the Side of the Vast Supplies of Nature. Crown 8vo, 5*s*.

LANDON, Joseph.—**School Management**; Including a General View of the Work of Education, Organization, and Discipline. Sixth Edition. Crown 8vo, 6*s*.

LAURIE, S. S.—**The Rise and Early Constitution of Universities.** With a Survey of Mediæval Education. Crown 8vo, 6*s*.

LEE, Rev. F. G., D.C.L.—**The Other World**; or, Glimpses of the Supernatural. 2 vols. A New Edition. Crown 8vo, 15*s*.

LEFEVRE, Right Hon. G. Shaw.—**Peel and O'Connell.** Demy 8vo, 10*s*. 6*d*.

Letters from an Unknown Friend. By the Author of "Charles Lowder." With a Preface by the Rev. W. H. CLEAVER. Fcap. 8vo, 1*s*.

Life of a Prig. By ONE. Third Edition. Fcap. 8vo, 3*s*. 6*d*.

LILLIE, Arthur, M.R.A.S.—**The Popular Life of Buddha.** Containing an Answer to the Hibbert Lectures of 1881. With Illustrations. Crown 8vo, 6*s*.

Buddhism in Christendom; or, Jesus the Essene. With Illustrations. Demy 8vo, 15*s*.

LONGFELLOW, H. Wadsworth.—**Life.** By his Brother, SAMUEL LONGFELLOW. With Portraits and Illustrations. 3 vols. Demy 8vo, 42*s*.

LONSDALE, Margaret.—**Sister Dora**: a Biography. With Portrait. Twenty-ninth Edition. Small crown 8vo, 2*s*. 6*d*.

George Eliot: Thoughts upon her Life, her Books, and Herself. Second Edition. Small crown 8vo, 1*s*. 6*d*.

LOUNSBURY, Thomas R.—**James Fenimore Cooper.** With Portrait. Crown 8vo, 5*s*.

LOWDER, Charles.—**A Biography.** By the Author of "St. Teresa." Twelfth Edition. Crown 8vo. With Portrait. 3*s*. 6*d*.

LÜCKES, Eva C. E.—**Lectures on General Nursing,** delivered to the Probationers of the London Hospital Training School for Nurses. Second Edition. Crown 8vo, 2*s*. 6*d*.

LYALL, William Rowe, D.D.—**Propædeia Prophetica**; or, The Use and Design of the Old Testament Examined. New Edition. With Notices by GEORGE C. PEARSON, M.A., Hon. Canon of Canterbury. Demy 8vo, 10*s*. 6*d*.

LYTTON, Edward Bulwer, Lord.—**Life, Letters and Literary Remains.** By his Son, the EARL OF LYTTON. With Portraits, Illustrations and Facsimiles. Demy 8vo. Vols. I. and II., 32*s*.

MACAULAY, G. C.—**Francis Beaumont: A Critical Study.** Crown 8vo, 5s.

MACHIAVELLI, Niccolò.—**Life and Times.** By Prof. VILLARI. Translated by LINDA VILLARI. 4 vols. Large post 8vo, 48s.

Discourses on the First Decade of Titus Livius. Translated from the Italian by NINIAN HILL THOMSON, M.A. Large crown 8vo, 12s.

The Prince. Translated from the Italian by N. H. T. Small crown 8vo, printed on hand-made paper, bevelled boards, 6s.

MACNEILL, J. G. Swift.—**How the Union was carried.** Crown 8vo, cloth, 1s. 6d.; paper covers, 1s.

MAGNUS, Lady.—**About the Jews since Bible Times.** From the Babylonian Exile till the English Exodus. Small crown 8vo, 6s.

MAGUIRE, Thomas.—**Lectures on Philosophy.** Demy 8vo, 9s.

Many Voices. A volume of Extracts from the Religious Writers of Christendom from the First to the Sixteenth Century. With Biographical Sketches. Crown 8vo, cloth extra, red edges, 6s.

MARKHAM, Capt. Albert Hastings, R.N.—**The Great Frozen Sea:** A Personal Narrative of the Voyage of the *Alert* during the Arctic Expedition of 1875-6. With 6 full-page Illustrations, 2 Maps, and 27 Woodcuts. Sixth and Cheaper Edition. Crown 8vo, 6s.

MARTINEAU, Gertrude.—**Outline Lessons on Morals.** Small crown 8vo, 3s. 6d.

MASON, Charlotte M.—**Home Education;** a Course of Lectures to Ladies. Crown 8vo, 3s. 6d.

Matter and Energy: An Examination of the Fundamental Conceptions of Physical Force. By B. L. L. Small crown 8vo, 2s.

MAUDSLEY, H., M.D.—**Body and Will.** Being an Essay concerning Will, in its Metaphysical, Physiological, and Pathological Aspects. 8vo, 12s.

Natural Causes and Supernatural Seemings. Second Edition. Crown 8vo, 6s.

McGRATH, Terence.—**Pictures from Ireland.** New and Cheaper Edition. Crown 8vo, 2s.

MEREDITH, M.A.—**Theotokos, the Example for Woman.** Dedicated, by permission, to Lady Agnes Wood. Revised by the Venerable Archdeacon DENISON. 32mo, limp cloth, 1s. 6d.

MILLER, Edward.—**The History and Doctrines of Irvingism;** or, The so-called Catholic and Apostolic Church. 2 vols. Large post 8vo, 15s.

The Church in Relation to the State. Large crown 8vo, 4s.

MILLS, *Herbert.*—**Poverty and the State**; or, Work for the Unemployed. An Inquiry into the Causes and Extent of Enforced Idleness, with a Statement of a Remedy. Crown 8vo, 6s.

MITCHELL, *Lucy M.*—**A History of Ancient Sculpture.** With numerous Illustrations, including 6 Plates in Phototype. Super-royal 8vo, 42s.

MOCKLER, *E.*—**A Grammar of the Baloochee Language**, as it is spoken in Makran (Ancient Gedrosia), in the Persia-Arabic and Roman characters. Fcap. 8vo, 5s.

MOHL, *Julius and Mary.*—**Letters and Recollections of.** By M. C. M. SIMPSON. With Portraits and Two Illustrations. Demy 8vo, 15s.

MOLESWORTH, *Rev. W. Nassau, M.A.*—**History of the Church of England from 1660.** Large crown 8vo, 7s. 6d.

MORELL, *J. R.*—**Euclid Simplified in Method and Language.** Being a Manual of Geometry. Compiled from the most important French Works, approved by the University of Paris and the Minister of Public Instruction. Fcap. 8vo, 2s. 6d.

MORGAN, *C. Lloyd.*—**The Springs of Conduct.** An Essay in Evolution. Large crown 8vo, cloth, 7s. 6d.

MORISON, *J. Cotter.*—**The Service of Man**: an Essay towards the Religion of the Future. Second Edition. Demy 8vo, 10s. 6d.

MORSE, *E. S., Ph.D.*—**First Book of Zoology.** With numerous Illustrations. New and Cheaper Edition. Crown 8vo, 2s. 6d.

My Lawyer: A Concise Abridgment of the Laws of England. By a Barrister-at-Law. Crown 8vo, 6s. 6d.

NELSON, *J. H., M.A.*—**A Prospectus of the Scientific Study of the Hindû Law.** Demy 8vo, 9s.

Indian Usage and Judge-made Law in Madras. Demy 8vo, 12s.

NEWMAN, *Cardinal.*—**Characteristics from the Writings of.** Being Selections from his various Works. Arranged with the Author's personal Approval. Seventh Edition. With Portrait. Crown 8vo, 6s.

* A Portrait of Cardinal Newman, mounted for framing, can be had, 2s. 6d.

NEWMAN, *Francis William.*—**Essays on Diet.** Small crown 8vo, cloth limp, 2s.

New Social Teachings. By POLITICUS. Small crown 8vo, 5s.

NICOLS, *Arthur, F.G.S., F.R.G.S.*—**Chapters from the Physical History of the Earth**: an Introduction to Geology and Palæontology. With numerous Illustrations. Crown 8vo, 5s.

NIHILL, *Rev. H. D.*—**The Sisters of St. Mary at the Cross**: Sisters of the Poor and their Work. Crown 8vo, 2s. 6d.

c

NOEL, The Hon. Roden.—Essays on Poetry and Poets. Demy 8vo, 12s.

NOPS, Marianne.—Class Lessons on Euclid. Part I. containing the First Two Books of the Elements. Crown 8vo, 2s. 6d.

Nuces: Exercises on the Syntax of the Public School Latin Primer. New Edition in Three Parts. Crown 8vo, each 1s.

*** The Three Parts can also be had bound together, 3s.

OATES, Frank, F.R.G.S.—Matabele Land and the Victoria Falls. A Naturalist's Wanderings in the Interior of South Africa. Edited by C. G. Oates, B.A. With numerous Illustrations and 4 Maps. Demy 8vo, 21s.

O'BRIEN, R. Barry.—Irish Wrongs and English Remedies, with other Essays. Crown 8vo, 5s.

OGLE, Anna C.—A Lost Love. Small crown 8vo, 2s. 6d.

O'MEARA, Kathleen.—Henri Perreyve and his Counsels to the Sick. Small crown 8vo, 5s.

One and a Half in Norway. A Chronicle of Small Beer. By Either and Both. Small crown 8vo, 3s. 6d.

O'NEIL, the late Rev. Lord.—Sermons. With Memoir and Portrait. Crown 8vo, 6s.

Essays and Addresses. Crown 8vo, 5s.

OTTLEY, H. Bickersteth.—The Great Dilemma. Christ His Own Witness or His Own Accuser. Six Lectures. Second Edition. Crown 8vo, 3s. 6d.

Our Public Schools—Eton, Harrow, Winchester, Rugby, Westminster, Marlborough, The Charterhouse. Crown 8vo, 6s.

PADGHAM, Richard.—In the Midst of Life we are in Death. Crown 8vo, 5s.

PALMER, the late William.—Notes of a Visit to Russia in 1840-1841. Selected and arranged by John H. Cardinal Newman, with Portrait. Crown 8vo, 8s. 6d.

Early Christian Symbolism. A Series of Compositions from Fresco Paintings, Glasses, and Sculptured Sarcophagi. Edited by the Rev. Provost Northcote, D.D., and the Rev. Canon Brownlow, M.A. With Coloured Plates, folio, 42s., or with Plain Plates, folio, 25s.

Parchment Library. Choicely Printed on hand-made paper, limp parchment antique or cloth, 6s. ; vellum, 7s. 6d. each volume.

The Poetical Works of John Milton. 2 vols.

Chaucer's Canterbury Tales. Edited by A. W. Pollard. 2 vols.

Parchment Library—*continued.*

- Letters and Journals of Jonathan Swift. Selected and edited, with a Commentary and Notes, by STANLEY LANE POOLE.
- De Quincey's Confessions of an English Opium Eater. Reprinted from the First Edition. Edited by RICHARD GARNETT.
- The Gospel according to Matthew, Mark, and Luke.
- Selections from the Prose Writings of Jonathan Swift. With a Preface and Notes by STANLEY LANE-POOLE and Portrait.
- English Sacred Lyrics.
- Sir Joshua Reynolds's Discourses. Edited by EDMUND GOSSE.
- Selections from Milton's Prose Writings. Edited by ERNEST MYERS.
- The Book of Psalms. Translated by the Rev. Canon T. K. CHEYNE, M.A., D.D.
- The Vicar of Wakefield. With Preface and Notes by AUSTIN DOBSON.
- English Comic Dramatists. Edited by OSWALD CRAWFURD.
- English Lyrics.
- The Sonnets of John Milton. Edited by MARK PATTISON. With Portrait after Vertue.
- French Lyrics. Selected and Annotated by GEORGE SAINTSBURY. With a Miniature Frontispiece designed and etched by H. G. Glindoni.
- Fables by Mr. John Gay. With Memoir by AUSTIN DOBSON, and an Etched Portrait from an unfinished Oil Sketch by Sir Godfrey Kneller.
- Select Letters of Percy Bysshe Shelley. Edited, with an Introduction, by RICHARD GARNETT.
- The Christian Year. Thoughts in Verse for the Sundays and Holy Days throughout the Year. With Miniature Portrait of the Rev. J. Keble, after a Drawing by G. Richmond, R.A.
- Shakspere's Works. Complete in Twelve Volumes.
- Eighteenth Century Essays. Selected and Edited by AUSTIN DOBSON. With a Miniature Frontispiece by R. Caldecott.
- Q. Horati Flacci Opera. Edited by F. A. CORNISH, Assistant Master at Eton. With a Frontispiece after a design by L. Alma Tadema, etched by Leopold Lowenstam.
- Edgar Allan Poe's Poems. With an Essay on his Poetry by ANDREW LANG, and a Frontispiece by Linley Sambourne.

Parchment Library—*continued.*

> Shakspere's Sonnets. Edited by EDWARD DOWDEN. With a Frontispiece etched by Leopold Lowenstam, after the Death Mask.
>
> English Odes. Selected by EDMUND GOSSE. With Frontispiece on India paper by Hamo Thornycroft, A.R.A.
>
> Of the Imitation of Christ. By THOMAS à KEMPIS. A revised Translation. With Frontispiece on India paper, from a Design by W. B. Richmond.
>
> Poems: Selected from PERCY BYSSHE SHELLEY. Dedicated to Lady Shelley. With a Preface by RICHARD GARNETT and a Miniature Frontispiece.

PARSLOE, Joseph.—Our Railways. Sketches, Historical and Descriptive. With Practical Information as to Fares and Rates, etc., and a Chapter on Railway Reform. Crown 8vo, 6s.

PASCAL, Blaise.—The Thoughts of. Translated from the Text of Auguste Molinier, by C. KEGAN PAUL. Large crown 8vo, with Frontispiece, printed on hand-made paper, parchment antique, or cloth, 12s.; vellum, 15s.

PAUL, Alexander.—Short Parliaments. A History of the National Demand for frequent General Elections. Small crown 8vo, 3s. 6d.

PAUL, C. Kegan.—Biographical Sketches. Printed on hand-made paper, bound in buckram. Second Edition. Crown 8vo, 7s. 6d.

PEARSON, Rev. S.—Week-day Living. A Book for Young Men and Women. Second Edition. Crown 8vo, 5s.

PENRICE, Major J.—Arabic and English Dictionary of the Koran. 4to, 21s.

PESCHEL, Dr. Oscar.—The Races of Man and their Geographical Distribution. Second Edition. Large crown 8vo, 9s.

PIDGEON, D.—An Engineer's Holiday; or, Notes of a Round Trip from Long. 0° to 0°. New and Cheaper Edition. Large crown 8vo, 7s. 6d.

> Old World Questions and New World Answers. Second Edition. Large crown 8vo, 7s. 6d.

Plain Thoughts for Men. Eight Lectures delivered at Forester's Hall, Clerkenwell, during the London Mission, 1884. Crown 8vo, cloth, 1s. 6d; paper covers, 1s.

PRICE, Prof. Bonamy.—Chapters on Practical Political Economy. Being the Substance of Lectures delivered before the University of Oxford. New and Cheaper Edition. Crown 8vo, 5s.

Prig's Bede: the Venerable Bede, Expurgated, Expounded, and Exposed. By The Prig. Second Edition. Fcap. 8vo, 3s. 6d.

Pulpit Commentary, The. (*Old Testament Series.*) Edited by the Rev. J. S. EXELL, M.A., and the Very Rev. Dean H. D. M. SPENCE, M.A., D.D.

- **Genesis.** By the Rev. T. WHITELAW, D.D. With Homilies by the Very Rev. J. F. MONTGOMERY, D.D., Rev. Prof. R. A. REDFORD, M.A., LL.B., Rev. F. HASTINGS, Rev. W. ROBERTS, M.A. An Introduction to the Study of the Old Testament by the Venerable Archdeacon FARRAR, D.D., F.R.S.; and Introductions to the Pentateuch by the Right Rev. H. COTTERILL, D.D., and Rev. T. WHITELAW, M.A. Eighth Edition. 1 vol., 15s.

- **Exodus.** By the Rev. Canon RAWLINSON. With Homilies by Rev. J. ORR, Rev. D. YOUNG, B.A., Rev. C. A. GOODHART, Rev. J. URQUHART, and the Rev. H. T. ROBJOHNS. Fourth Edition. 2 vols., 18s.

- **Leviticus.** By the Rev. Prebendary MEYRICK, M.A. With Introductions by the Rev. R. COLLINS, Rev. Professor A. CAVE, and Homilies by Rev. Prof. REDFORD, LL.B., Rev. J. A. MACDONALD, Rev. W. CLARKSON, B.A., Rev. S. R. ALDRIDGE, LL.B., and Rev. MCCHEYNE EDGAR. Fourth Edition. 15s.

- **Numbers.** By the Rev. R. WINTERBOTHAM, LL.B. With Homilies by the Rev. Professor W. BINNIE, D.D., Rev. E. S. PROUT, M.A., Rev. D. YOUNG, Rev. J. WAITE, and an Introduction by the Rev. THOMAS WHITELAW, M.A. Fifth Edition. 15s.

- **Deuteronomy.** By the Rev. W. L. ALEXANDER, D.D. With Homilies by Rev. C. CLEMANCE, D.D., Rev. J. ORR, B.D., Rev. R. M. EDGAR, M.A., Rev. D. DAVIES, M.A. Fourth edition. 15s.

- **Joshua.** By Rev. J. J. LIAS, M.A. With Homilies by Rev. S. R. ALDRIDGE, LL.B., Rev. R. GLOVER, REV. E. DE PRESSENSÉ, D.D., Rev. J. WAITE, B.A., Rev. W. F. ADENEY, M.A.; and an Introduction by the Rev. A. PLUMMER, M.A. Fifth Edition. 12s. 6d.

- **Judges and Ruth.** By the Bishop of BATH and WELLS, and Rev. J. MORISON, D.D. With Homilies by Rev. A. F. MUIR, M.A., Rev. W. F. ADENEY, M.A., Rev. W. M. STATHAM, and Rev. Professor J. THOMSON, M.A. Fifth Edition. 10s. 6d.

- **1 Samuel.** By the Very Rev. R. P. SMITH, D.D. With Homilies by Rev. DONALD FRASER, D.D., Rev. Prof. CHAPMAN, and Rev. B. DALE. Sixth Edition. 15s.

- **1 Kings.** By the Rev. JOSEPH HAMMOND, LL.B. With Homilies by the Rev. E. DE PRESSENSÉ, D.D., Rev. J. WAITE, B.A., Rev. A. ROWLAND, LL.B., Rev. J. A. MACDONALD, and Rev. J. URQUHART. Fifth Edition. 15s.

Pulpit Commentary, The—*continued.*

1 Chronicles. By the Rev. Prof. P. C. BARKER, M.A., LL.B. With Homilies by Rev. Prof. J. R. THOMSON, M.A., Rev. R. TUCK, B.A., Rev. W. CLARKSON, B.A., Rev. F. WHITFIELD, M.A., and Rev. RICHARD GLOVER. 15s.

Ezra, Nehemiah, and Esther. By Rev. Canon G. RAWLINSON, M.A. With Homilies by Rev. Prof. J. R. THOMSON, M.A., Rev. Prof. R. A. REDFORD, LL.B., M.A., Rev. W. S. LEWIS, M.A., Rev. J. A. MACDONALD, Rev. A. MACKENNAL, B.A., Rev. W. CLARKSON, B.A., Rev. F. HASTINGS, Rev. W. DINWIDDIE, LL.B., Rev. Prof. ROWLANDS, B.A., Rev. G. WOOD, B.A., Rev. Prof. P. C. BARKER, M.A., LL.B., and the Rev. J. S. EXELL, M.A. Sixth Edition. 1 vol., 12s. 6d.

Isaiah. By the Rev. Canon G. RAWLINSON, M.A. With Homilies by Rev. Prof. E. JOHNSON, M.A., Rev. W. CLARKSON, B.A., Rev. W. M. STATHAM, and Rev. R. TUCK, B.A. Second Edition. 2 vols., 15s. each.

Jeremiah. (Vol. I.) By the Rev. Canon T. K. CHEYNE, M.A., D.D. With Homilies by the Rev. W. F. ADENEY, M.A., Rev. A. F. MUIR, M.A., Rev. S. CONWAY, B.A., Rev. J. WAITE, B.A., and Rev. D. YOUNG, B.A. Third Edition. 15s.

Jeremiah (Vol. II.) and Lamentations. By Rev. T. K. CHEYNE, M.A. With Homilies by Rev. Prof. J. R. THOMSON, M.A., Rev. W. F. ADENEY, M.A., Rev. A. F. MUIR, M.A., Rev. S. CONWAY, B.A., Rev. D. YOUNG, B.A. 15s.

Hosea and Joel. By the Rev. Prof. J. J. GIVEN, Ph.D., D.D. With Homilies by the Rev. Prof. J. R. THOMSON, M.A., Rev. A. ROWLAND, B.A., LL.B., Rev. C. JERDAN, M.A., LL.B., Rev. J. ORR, M.A., B.D., and Rev. D. THOMAS, D.D. 15s.

Pulpit Commentary, The. (*New Testament Series.*)

St. Mark. By Very Rev. E. BICKERSTETH, D.D., Dean of Lichfield. With Homilies by Rev. Prof. THOMSON, M.A., Rev. Prof. J. J. GIVEN, Ph.D., D.D., Rev. Prof. JOHNSON, M.A., Rev. A. ROWLAND, B.A., LL.B., Rev. A. MUIR, and Rev. R. GREEN. Fifth Edition. 2 vols., 21s.

The Acts of the Apostles. By the Bishop of BATH and WELLS. With Homilies by Rev. Prof. P. C. BARKER, M.A., LL.B., Rev. Prof. E. JOHNSON, M.A., Rev. Prof. R. A. REDFORD, LL.B., Rev. R. TUCK, B.A., Rev. W. CLARKSON, B.A. Third Edition. 2 vols., 21s.

1 Corinthians. By the Ven. Archdeacon FARRAR, D.D. With Homilies by Rev. Ex-Chancellor LIPSCOMB, LL.D., Rev. DAVID THOMAS, D.D., Rev. D. FRASER, D.D., Rev. Prof. J. R. THOMSON, M.A., Rev. J. WAITE, B.A., Rev. R. TUCK, B.A., Rev. E. HURNDALL, M.A., and Rev. H. BREMNER, B.D. Third Edition. 15s.

Pulpit Commentary, The—*continued.*

> **2 Corinthians and Galatians.** By the Ven. Archdeacon FARRAR, D.D., and Rev. Prebendary E. HUXTABLE. With Homilies by Rev. Ex-Chancellor LIPSCOMB, LL.D., Rev. DAVID THOMAS, D.D., Rev. DONALD FRASER, D.D., Rev. R. TUCK, B.A., Rev. E. HURNDALL, M.A., Rev. Prof. J. R. THOMSON, M.A., Rev. R. FINLAYSON, B.A., Rev. W. F. ADENEY, M.A., Rev. R. M. EDGAR, M.A., and Rev. T. CROSKERY, D.D. 21s.
>
> **Ephesians, Philippians, and Colossians.** By the Rev. Prof. W. G. BLAIKIE, D.D., Rev. B. C. CAFFIN, M.A., and Rev. G. G. FINDLAY, B.A. With Homilies by Rev. D. THOMAS, D.D., Rev. R. M. EDGAR, M.A., Rev. R. FINLAYSON, B.A., Rev. W. F. ADENEY, M.A., Rev. Prof. T. CROSKERY, D.D., Rev. E. S. PROUT, M.A., Rev. Canon VERNON HUTTON, and Rev. U. R. THOMAS, D.D. Second Edition. 21s.
>
> **Thessalonians, Timothy, Titus, and Philemon.** By the Bishop of Bath and Wells, Rev. Dr. GLOAG and Rev. Dr. EALES. With Homilies by the Rev. B. C. CAFFIN, M.A., Rev. R. FINLAYSON, B.A., Rev. Prof. T. CROSKERY, D.D., Rev. W. F. ADENEY, M.A., Rev. W. M. STATHAM, and Rev. D. THOMAS, D.D. 15s.
>
> **Hebrews and James.** By the Rev. J. BARMBY, D.D., and Rev Prebendary E. C. S. GIBSON, M.A. With Homiletics by the Rev. C. JERDAN, M.A., LL.B., and Rev. Prebendary E. C. S. GIBSON. And Homilies by the Rev. W. JONES, Rev. C. NEW, Rev. D. YOUNG, B.A., Rev. J. S. BRIGHT, Rev. T. F. LOCKYER, B.A., and Rev. C. JERDAN, M.A., LL.B. Second Edition. 15s.

PUSEY, Dr.—**Sermons for the Church's Seasons from Advent to Trinity.** Selected from the Published Sermons of the late EDWARD BOUVERIE PUSEY, D.D. Crown 8vo, 5s.

RANKE, Leopold von.—**Universal History.** The oldest Historical Group of Nations and the Greeks. Edited by G. W. PROTHERO. Demy 8vo, 16s.

RENDELL, J. M.—**Concise Handbook of the Island of Madeira.** With Plan of Funchal and Map of the Island. Fcap. 8vo, 1s. 6d.

REVELL, W. F.—**Ethical Forecasts.** Crown 8vo.

REYNOLDS, Rev. J. W.—**The Supernatural in Nature.** A Verification by Free Use of Science. Third Edition, Revised and Enlarged. Demy 8vo, 14s.

> **The Mystery of Miracles.** Third and Enlarged Edition. Crown 8vo, 6s.
>
> **The Mystery of the Universe our Common Faith.** Demy 8vo, 14s.
>
> **The World to Come:** Immortality a Physical Fact. Crown 8vo, 6s.

RIBOT, *Prof. Th.*—Heredity: A Psychological Study of its Phenomena, its Laws, its Causes, and its Consequences. Second Edition. Large crown 8vo, 9s.

ROBERTSON, *The late Rev. F. W., M.A.*—Life and Letters of. Edited by the Rev. STOPFORD BROOKE, M.A.
    I. Two vols., uniform with the Sermons. With Steel Portrait. Crown 8vo, 7s. 6d.
    II. Library Edition, in Demy 8vo, with Portrait. 12s.
    III. A Popular Edition, in 1 vol. Crown 8vo, 6s.

ROBERTSON, *The late Rev. F. W., M.A.*—*continued.*
    Sermons. Four Series. Small crown 8vo, 3s. 6d. each.
    The Human Race, and other Sermons. Preached at Cheltenham, Oxford, and Brighton. New and Cheaper Edition. Small crown 8vo, 3s. 6d.
    Notes on Genesis. New and Cheaper Edition. Small crown 8vo, 3s. 6d.
    Expository Lectures on St. Paul's Epistles to the Corinthians. A New Edition. Small crown 8vo, 5s.
    Lectures and Addresses, with other Literary Remains. A New Edition. Small crown 8vo, 5s.
    An Analysis of Tennyson's "In Memoriam." (Dedicated by Permission to the Poet-Laureate.) Fcap. 8vo, 2s.
    The Education of the Human Race. Translated from the German of GOTTHOLD EPHRAIM LESSING. Fcap. 8vo, 2s. 6d.
    The above Works can also be had, bound in half morocco.

  *** A Portrait of the late Rev. F. W. Robertson, mounted for framing, can be had, 2s. 6d.

ROMANES, *G. J.*—Mental Evolution in Animals. With a Posthumous Essay on Instinct by CHARLES DARWIN, F.R.S. Demy 8vo, 12s.

ROOSEVELT, *Theodore.* Hunting Trips of a Ranchman. Sketches of Sport on the Northern Cattle Plains. With 26 Illustrations. Royal 8vo, 18s.

ROSMINI SERBATI, *Antonio.*—Life. By the REV. W. LOCKHART. Second Edition. 2 vols. With Portraits. Crown 8vo, 12s.

Rosmini's Origin of Ideas. Translated from the Fifth Italian Edition of the Nuovo Saggio *Sull' origine delle idee*. 3 vols. Demy 8vo, cloth, 10s. 6d. each.

Rosmini's Psychology. 3 vols. Demy 8vo [Vols. I. and II. now ready], 10s. 6d. each.

ROSS, *Janet.*—Italian Sketches. With 14 full-page Illustrations. Crown 8vo, 7s. 6d.

RULE, *Martin, M.A.*—The Life and Times of St. Anselm, Archbishop of Canterbury and Primate of the Britains. 2 vols. Demy 8vo, 32s.

SAMUELL, *Richard.*—**Seven, the Sacred Number**: Its use in Scripture and its Application to Biblical Criticism. Crown 8vo, 10s. 6d.

SAYCE, *Rev. Archibald Henry.*—**Introduction to the Science of Language.** 2 vols. Second Edition. Large post 8vo, 21s.

SCOONES, *W. Baptiste.*—**Four Centuries of English Letters:** A Selection of 350 Letters by 150 Writers, from the Period of the Paston Letters to the Present Time. Third Edition. Large crown 8vo, 6s.

SÉE, *Prof. Germain.*—**Bacillary Phthisis of the Lungs.** Translated and edited for English Practitioners by WILLIAM HENRY WEDDELL, M.R.C.S. Demy 8vo, 10s. 6d.

Shakspere's Works. The Avon Edition, 12 vols., fcap. 8vo, cloth, 18s.; in cloth box, 21s.; bound in 6 vols., cloth, 15s.

Shakspere's Works, an Index to. By EVANGELINE O'CONNOR. Crown 8vo, 5s.

SHELLEY, *Percy Bysshe.*—**Life.** By EDWARD DOWDEN, LL.D. 2 vols. With Portraits. Demy 8vo, 36s.

SHILLITO, *Rev. Joseph.*—**Womanhood**: its Duties, Temptations, and Privileges. A Book for Young Women. Third Edition. Crown 8vo, 3s. 6d.

Shooting, Practical Hints. Being a Treatise on the Shot Gun and its Management. By "20 Bore." With 55 Illustrations. Demy 8vo, 12s.

Sister Augustine, Superior of the Sisters of Charity at the St. Johannis Hospital at Bonn. Authorized Translation by HANS THARAU, from the German "Memorials of AMALIE VON LASAULX." Cheap Edition. Large crown 8vo, 4s. 6d.

SKINNER, *James.*—**A Memoir.** By the Author of "Charles Lowder." With a Preface by the Rev. Canon CARTER, and Portrait. Large crown, 7s. 6d.

_{*} Also a cheap Edition. With Portrait. Fourth Edition. Crown 8vo, 3s. 6d.

SMEATON, *D. Mackenzie.*—**The Loyal Karens of Burma.** Crown 8vo, 4s. 6d.

SMITH, *Edward, M.D., LL.B., F.R.S.*—**Tubercular Consumption in its Early and Remediable Stages.** Second Edition. Crown 8vo, 6s.

SMITH, *Sir W. Cusack, Bart.*—**Our War Ships.** A Naval Essay. Crown 8vo, 5s.

Spanish Mystics. By the Editor of "Many Voices." Crown 8vo, 5s.

Specimens of English Prose Style from Malory to Macaulay. Selected and Annotated, with an Introductory Essay, by GEORGE SAINTSBURY. Large crown 8vo, printed on hand-made paper, parchment antique or cloth, 12s.; vellum, 15s.

SPEDDING, James.—**Reviews and Discussions, Literary, Political, and Historical not relating to Bacon.** Demy 8vo, 12s. 6d.

Evenings with a Reviewer; or, Macaulay and Bacon. With a Prefatory Notice by G. S. VENABLES, Q.C. 2 vols. Demy 8vo, 18s.

Stray Papers on Education, and Scenes from School Life. By B. H. Second Edition. Small crown 8vo, 3s. 6d.

STREATFEILD, Rev. G. S., M.A.—**Lincolnshire and the Danes.** Large crown 8vo, 7s. 6d.

STRECKER-WISLICENUS.—**Organic Chemistry.** Translated and Edited, with Extensive Additions, by W. R. HODGKINSON, Ph.D., and A. J. GREENAWAY, F.I.C. Second and cheaper Edition. Demy 8vo, 12s. 6d.

Suakin, 1885; being a Sketch of the Campaign of this year. By an Officer who was there. Second Edition. Crown 8vo, 2s. 6d.

SULLY, James, M.A.—**Pessimism:** a History and a Criticism. Second Edition. Demy 8vo, 14s.

Sunshine and Sea. A Yachting Visit to the Channel Islands and Coast of Brittany. With Frontispiece from a Photograph and 24 Illustrations. Crown 8vo, 6s.

SWEDENBORG, Eman.—**De Cultu et Amore Dei ubi Agitur de Telluris ortu, Paradiso et Vivario, tum de Primogeniti Seu Adami Nativitate Infantia, et Amore.** Crown 8vo, 6s.

On the Worship and Love of God. Treating of the Birth of the Earth, Paradise, and the Abode of Living Creatures. Translated from the original Latin. Crown 8vo, 7s. 6d.

Prodromus Philosophiæ Ratiocinantis de Infinito, et Causa Finali Creationis: deque Mechanismo Operationis Animæ et Corporis. Edidit THOMAS MURRAY GORMAN, M.A. Crown 8vo, 7s. 6d.

TACITUS.—**The Agricola.** A Translation. Small crown 8vo, 2s. 6d.

TARRING, C. J.—**A Practical Elementary Turkish Grammar.** Crown 8vo, 6s.

TAYLOR, Rev. Isaac.—**The Alphabet.** An Account of the Origin and Development of Letters. With numerous Tables and Facsimiles. 2 vols. Demy 8vo, 36s.

TAYLOR, Jeremy.—**The Marriage Ring.** With Preface, Notes, and Appendices. Edited by FRANCIS BURDETT MONEY COUTTS. Small crown 8vo, 2s. 6d.

TAYLOR, Sedley.—**Profit Sharing between Capital and Labour.** To which is added a Memorandum on the Industrial Partnership at the Whitwood Collieries, by ARCHIBALD and HENRY BRIGGS, with remarks by SEDLEY TAYLOR. Crown 8vo, 2s. 6d.

THOM, *J. Hamilton.*—**Laws of Life after the Mind of Christ.** Two Series. Crown 8vo, 7*s.* 6*d.* each.

THOMPSON, *Sir H.*—**Diet in Relation to Age and Activity.** Fcap. 8vo, cloth, 1*s.* 6*d.* ; paper covers, 1*s.*

TIDMAN, *Paul F.*—**Money and Labour.** 1*s.* 6*d.*

TIPPLE, *Rev. S. A.*—**Sunday Mornings at Norwood.** Prayers and Sermons. Crown 8vo, 6*s.*

TODHUNTER, *Dr. J.*—**A Study of Shelley.** Crown 8vo, 7*s.*

TOLSTOI, *Count Leo.*—**Christ's Christianity.** Translated from the Russian. Large crown 8vo, 7*s.* 6*d.*

TRANT, *William.*—**Trade Unions; Their Origin, Objects, and Efficacy.** Small crown 8vo, 1*s.* 6*d.* ; paper covers, 1*s.*

TRENCH, *The late R. C., Archbishop.*—**Notes on the Parables of Our Lord.** Fourteenth Edition. 8vo, 12*s.* Cheap Edition, 7*s.* 6*d.*

Notes on the Miracles of Our Lord. Twelfth Edition. 8vo, 12*s.* Cheap Edition, 7*s.* 6*d.*

Studies in the Gospels. Fifth Edition, Revised. 8vo, 10*s.* 6*d.*

Brief Thoughts and Meditations on Some Passages in Holy Scripture. Third Edition. Crown 8vo, 3*s.* 6*d.*

Synonyms of the New Testament. Tenth Edition, Enlarged. 8vo, 12*s.*

Sermons New and Old. Crown 8vo, 6*s.*

On the Authorized Version of the New Testament. Second Edition. 8vo, 7*s.*

Commentary on the Epistles to the Seven Churches in Asia. Fourth Edition, Revised. 8vo, 8*s.* 6*d.*

The Sermon on the Mount. An Exposition drawn from the Writings of St. Augustine, with an Essay on his Merits as an Interpreter of Holy Scripture. Fourth Edition, Enlarged. 8vo, 10*s.* 6*d.*

Shipwrecks of Faith. Three Sermons preached before the University of Cambridge in May, 1867. Fcap. 8vo, 2*s.* 6*d.*

Lectures on Mediæval Church History. Being the Substance of Lectures delivered at Queen's College, London. Second Edition. 8vo, 12*s.*

English, Past and Present. Thirteenth Edition, Revised and Improved. Fcap. 8vo, 5*s.*

On the Study of Words. Nineteenth Edition, Revised. Fcap. 8vo, 5*s.*

TRENCH, *The late R. C., Archbishop.—continued.*

Select Glossary of English Words Used Formerly in Senses Different from the Present. Sixth Edition, Revised and Enlarged. Fcap. 8vo, 5s.

Proverbs and Their Lessons. Seventh Edition, Enlarged. Fcap. 8vo, 4s.

Poems. Collected and Arranged anew. Ninth Edition. Fcap. 8vo, 7s. 6d.

Poems. Library Edition. 2 vols. Small crown 8vo, 10s.

Sacred Latin Poetry. Chiefly Lyrical, Selected and Arranged for Use. Third Edition, Corrected and Improved. Fcap. 8vo, 7s.

A Household Book of English Poetry. Selected and Arranged, with Notes. Fourth Edition, Revised. Extra fcap. 8vo, 5s. 6d.

An Essay on the Life and Genius of Calderon. With Translations from his "Life's a Dream" and "Great Theatre of the World." Second Edition, Revised and Improved. Extra fcap. 8vo, 5s. 6d.

Gustavus Adolphus in Germany, and other Lectures on the Thirty Years' War. Third Edition, Enlarged. Fcap. 8vo, 4s.

Plutarch: his Life, his Lives, and his Morals. Second Edition, Enlarged. Fcap. 8vo, 3s. 6d.

Remains of the late Mrs. Richard Trench. Being Selections from her Journals, Letters, and other Papers. New and Cheaper Issue. With Portrait. 8vo, 6s.

TUKE, *Daniel Hack, M.D., F.R.C.P.*—Chapters in the History of the Insane in the British Isles. With Four Illustrations. Large crown 8vo, 12s.

TWINING, *Louisa.*—Workhouse Visiting and Management during Twenty-Five Years. Small crown 8vo, 2s.

VAUGHAN, *H. Halford.*—New Readings and Renderings of Shakespeare's Tragedies. 3 vols. Demy 8vo, 12s. 6d. each.

VICARY, *J. Fulford.*—Saga Time. With Illustrations. Crown 8vo, 7s. 6d.

VOGT, *Lieut.-Col. Hermann.*—The Egyptian War of 1882. A translation. With Map and Plans. Large crown 8vo, 6s.

VOLCKXSOM, *E. W. v.*—Catechism of Elementary Modern Chemistry. Small crown 8vo, 3s.

WALPOLE, *Chas. George.*—A Short History of Ireland from the Earliest Times to the Union with Great Britain. With 5 Maps and Appendices. Third Edition. Crown 8vo, 6s.

WARD, *Wilfrid.*—**The Wish to Believe.** A Discussion Concerning the Temper of Mind in which a reasonable Man should undertake Religious Inquiry. Small crown 8vo, 5*s.*

WARD, *William George, Ph.D.*—**Essays on the Philosophy of Theism.** Edited, with an Introduction, by WILFRID WARD. 2 vols. Demy 8vo, 21*s.*

WARNER, *Francis, M.D.*—**Lectures on the Anatomy of Movement.** Crown 8vo, 4*s.* 6*d.*

WARTER, *J. W.*—**An Old Shropshire Oak.** 2 vols. Demy 8vo, 28*s.*

WEDMORE, *Frederick.*—**The Masters of Genre Painting.** With Sixteen Illustrations. Post 8vo, 7*s.* 6*d.*

WHITMAN, *Sidney.*—**Conventional Cant: its Results and Remedy.** Crown 8vo, 6*s.*

WHITNEY, *Prof. William Dwight.*—**Essentials of English Grammar,** for the Use of Schools. Second Edition. Crown 8vo, 3*s.* 6*d.*

WHITWORTH, *George Clifford.*—**An Anglo-Indian Dictionary:** a Glossary of Indian Terms used in English, and of such English or other Non-Indian Terms as have obtained special meanings in India. Demy 8vo, cloth, 12*s.*

WILSON, *Lieut.-Col. C. T.*—**The Duke of Berwick, Marshal of France, 1702-1734.** Demy 8vo, 15*s.*

WILSON, *Mrs. R. F.*—**The Christian Brothers.** Their Origin and Work. With a Sketch of the Life of their Founder, the Ven. JEAN BAPTISTE, de la Salle. Crown 8vo, 6*s.*

WOLTMANN, *Dr. Alfred, and* WOERMANN, *Dr. Karl.*—**History of Painting.** With numerous Illustrations. Medium 8vo. Vol. I. Painting in Antiquity and the Middle Ages. 28*s.*; bevelled boards, gilt leaves, 30*s.* Vol. II. The Painting of the Renascence. 42*s.*; bevelled boards, gilt leaves, 45*s.*

YOUMANS, *Edward L., M.D.*—**A Class Book of Chemistry,** on the Basis of the New System. With 200 Illustrations. Crown 8vo, 5*s.*

YOUMANS, *Eliza A.*—**First Book of Botany.** Designed to Cultivate the Observing Powers of Children. With 300 Engravings. New and Cheaper Edition. Crown 8vo, 2*s.* 6*d.*

YOUNG, *Arthur.*—**Axial Polarity of Man's Word-Embodied Ideas, and its Teaching.** Demy 4to, 15*s.*

THE INTERNATIONAL SCIENTIFIC SERIES.

I. **Forms of Water in Clouds and Rivers, Ice and Glaciers.** By J. Tyndall, LL.D., F.R.S. With 25 Illustrations. Ninth Edition. 5s.

II. **Physics and Politics**; or, Thoughts on the Application of the Principles of "Natural Selection" and "Inheritance" to Political Society. By Walter Bagehot. Eighth Edition. 4s.

III. **Foods.** By Edward Smith, M.D., LL.B., F.R.S. With numerous Illustrations. Ninth Edition. 5s.

IV. **Mind and Body**: the Theories and their Relation. By Alexander Bain, LL.D. With Four Illustrations. Eighth Edition. 4s.

V. **The Study of Sociology.** By Herbert Spencer. Thirteenth Edition. 5s.

VI. **On the Conservation of Energy.** By Balfour Stewart, M.A., LL.D., F.R.S. With 14 Illustrations. Seventh Edition. 5s.

VII. **Animal Locomotion**; or Walking, Swimming, and Flying. By J. B. Pettigrew, M.D., F.R.S., etc. With 130 Illustrations. Third Edition. 5s.

VIII. **Responsibility in Mental Disease.** By Henry Maudsley, M.D. Fourth Edition. 5s.

IX. **The New Chemistry.** By Professor J. P. Cooke. With 31 Illustrations. Ninth Edition. 5s.

X. **The Science of Law.** By Professor Sheldon Amos. Sixth Edition. 5s.

XI. **Animal Mechanism**: a Treatise on Terrestrial and Aerial Locomotion. By Professor E. J. Marey. With 117 Illustrations. Third Edition. 5s.

XII. **The Doctrine of Descent and Darwinism.** By Professor Oscar Schmidt. With 26 Illustrations. Seventh Edition. 5s.

XIII. **The History of the Conflict between Religion and Science.** By J. W. Draper, M.D., LL.D. Twentieth Edition. 5s.

XIV. **Fungi**: their Nature, Influences, Uses, etc. By M. C. Cooke, M.D., LL.D. Edited by the Rev. M. J. Berkeley, M.A., F.L.S. With numerous Illustrations. Third Edition. 5s.

XV. **The Chemical Effects of Light and Photography.** By Dr. Hermann Vogel. With 100 Illustrations. Fourth Edition. 5s.

XVI. **The Life and Growth of Language.** By Professor William Dwight Whitney. Fifth Edition. 5s.

XVII. **Money and the Mechanism of Exchange.** By W Stanley Jevons, M.A., F.R.S. Eighth Edition. 5*s.*

XVIII. **The Nature of Light.** With a General Account of Physical Optics. By Dr. Eugene Lommel. With 188 Illustrations and a Table of Spectra in Chromo-lithography. Fourth Edition. 5*s.*

XIX. **Animal Parasites and Messmates.** By P. J. Van Beneden. With 83 Illustrations. Third Edition. 5*s.*

XX. **Fermentation.** By Professor Schützenberger. With 28 Illustrations. Fourth Edition. 5*s.*

XXI. **The Five Senses of Man.** By Professor Bernstein. With 91 Illustrations. Fifth Edition. 5*s.*

XXII. **The Theory of Sound in its Relation to Music.** By Professor Pietro Blaserna. With numerous Illustrations. Third Edition. 5*s.*

XXIII. **Studies in Spectrum Analysis.** By J. Norman Lockyer, F.R.S. With six photographic Illustrations of Spectra, and numerous engravings on Wood. Fourth Edition. 6*s.* 6*d.*

XXIV. **A History of the Growth of the Steam Engine.** By Professor R. H. Thurston. With numerous Illustrations. Fourth Edition. 6*s.* 6*d.*

XXV. **Education as a Science.** By Alexander Bain, LL.D. Sixth Edition. 5*s.*

XXVI. **The Human Species.** By Professor A. de Quatrefages. Fourth Edition. 5*s.*

XXVII. **Modern Chromatics.** With Applications to Art and Industry. By Ogden N. Rood. With 130 original Illustrations. Second Edition. 5*s.*

XXVIII. **The Crayfish**: an Introduction to the Study of Zoology. By Professor T. H. Huxley. With 82 Illustrations. Fourth Edition. 5*s.*

XXIX. **The Brain as an Organ of Mind.** By H. Charlton Bastian, M.D. With numerous Illustrations. Third Edition. 5*s.*

XXX. **The Atomic Theory.** By Prof. Wurtz. Translated by G. Cleminshaw, F.C.S. Fourth Edition. 5*s.*

XXXI. **The Natural Conditions of Existence as they affect Animal Life.** By Karl Semper. With 2 Maps and 106 Woodcuts. Third Edition. 5*s.*

XXXII. **General Physiology of Muscles and Nerves.** By Prof. J. Rosenthal. Third Edition. With Illustrations. 5*s.*

XXXIII. **Sight**: an Exposition of the Principles of Monocular and Binocular Vision. By Joseph le Conte, LL.D. Second Edition. With 132 Illustrations. 5*s.*

XXXIV. **Illusions**: a Psychological Study. By James Sully. Third Edition. 5*s*.

XXXV. **Volcanoes: what they are and what they teach.** By Professor J. W. Judd, F.R.S. With 92 Illustrations on Wood. Third Edition. 5*s*.

XXXVI. **Suicide**: an Essay on Comparative Moral Statistics. By Prof. H. Morselli. Second Edition. With Diagrams. 5*s*.

XXXVII. **The Brain and its Functions.** By J. Luys. With Illustrations. Second Edition. 5*s*.

XXXVIII. **Myth and Science**: an Essay. By Tito Vignoli. Third Edition. 5*s*.

XXXIX. **The Sun.** By Professor Young. With Illustrations. Second Edition. 5*s*.

XL. **Ants, Bees, and Wasps**: a Record of Observations on the Habits of the Social Hymenoptera. By Sir John Lubbock, Bart., M.P. With 5 Chromo-lithographic Illustrations. Eighth Edition. 5*s*.

XLI. **Animal Intelligence.** By G. J. Romanes, LL.D., F.R.S. Fourth Edition. 5*s*.

XLII. **The Concepts and Theories of Modern Physics.** By J. B. Stallo. Third Edition. 5*s*.

XLIII. **Diseases of the Memory**; An Essay in the Positive Psychology. By Prof. Th. Ribot. Third Edition. 5*s*.

XLIV. **Man before Metals.** By N. Joly, with 148 Illustrations. Fourth Edition. 5*s*.

XLV. **The Science of Politics.** By Prof. Sheldon Amos. Third Edition. 5*s*.

XLVI. **Elementary Meteorology.** By Robert H. Scott. Fourth Edition. With Numerous Illustrations. 5*s*.

XLVII. **The Organs of Speech and their Application in the Formation of Articulate Sounds.** By Georg Hermann Von Meyer. With 47 Woodcuts. 5*s*.

XLVIII. **Fallacies.** A View of Logic from the Practical Side. By Alfred Sidgwick. Second Edition. 5*s*.

XLIX. **Origin of Cultivated Plants.** By Alphonse de Candolle. 5*s*.

L. **Jelly-Fish, Star-Fish, and Sea-Urchins.** Being a Research on Primitive Nervous Systems. By G. J. Romanes. With Illustrations. 5*s*.

LI. **The Common Sense of the Exact Sciences.** By the late William Kingdon Clifford. Second Edition. With 100 Figures. 5*s*.

LII. **Physical Expression: Its Modes and Principles.** By Francis Warner, M.D., F.R.C.P., Hunterian Professor of Comparative Anatomy and Physiology, R.C.S.E. With 50 Illustrations. 5*s*.

LIII. **Anthropoid Apes.** By Robert Hartmann. With 63 Illustrations. 5*s*.

LIV. **The Mammalia in their Relation to Primeval Times.** By Oscar Schmidt. With 51 Woodcuts. 5*s*.

LV. **Comparative Literature.** By H. Macaulay Posnett, LL.D. 5*s*.

LVI. **Earthquakes and other Earth Movements.** By Prof. John Milne. With 38 Figures. Second Edition. 5*s*.

LVII. **Microbes, Ferments, and Moulds.** By E. L. Trouessart. With 107 Illustrations. 5*s*.

LVIII. **Geographical and Geological Distribution of Animals.** By Professor A. Heilprin. With Frontispiece. 5*s*.

LIX. **Weather.** A Popular Exposition of the Nature of Weather Changes from Day to Day. By the Hon. Ralph Abercromby. With 96 Illustrations. 5*s*.

LX. **Animal Magnetism.** By Alfred Binet and Charles Féré. 5*s*.

LXI. **Manual of British Discomycetes,** with descriptions of all the Species of Fungi hitherto found in Britain included in the Family, and Illustrations of the Genera. By William Phillips, F.L.S. 5*s*.

LXII. **International Law.** With Materials for a Code of International Law. By Professor Leone Levi. 5*s*.

LXIII. **The Origin of Floral Structures through Insect Agency.** By Prof. G. Henslow.

MILITARY WORKS.

BRACKENBURY, Col. C. B., R.A.—Military Handbooks for Regimental Officers.

  I. **Military Sketching and Reconnaissance.** By Col. F. J. Hutchison and Major H. G. MacGregor. Fifth Edition. With 15 Plates. Small crown 8vo, 4*s*.

  II. **The Elements of Modern Tactics Practically applied to English Formations.** By Lieut.-Col. Wilkinson Shaw. Sixth Edition. With 25 Plates and Maps. Small crown 8vo, 9*s*.

  III. **Field Artillery.** Its Equipment, Organization and Tactics. By Major Sisson C. Pratt, R.A. With 12 Plates. Third Edition. Small crown 8vo, 6*s*.

BRACKENBURY, *Col. C. B., R.A.—continued.*

    IV. **The Elements of Military Administration.** First Part: Permanent System of Administration. By Major J. W. Buxton. Small crown 8vo, 7s. 6d.

    V. **Military Law:** Its Procedure and Practice. By Major Sisson C. Pratt, R.A. Third Edition. Small crown 8vo, 4s. 6d.

    VI. **Cavalry in Modern War.** By Col. F. Chenevix Trench. Small crown 8vo, 6s.

    VII. **Field Works.** Their Technical Construction and Tactical Application. By the Editor, Col. C. B. Brackenbury, R.A. Small crown 8vo.

BRENT, *Brig.-Gen. J. L.*—**Mobilizable Fortifications and their Controlling Influence in War.** Crown 8vo, 5s.

BROOKE, *Major, C. K.*—**A System of Field Training.** Small crown 8vo, cloth limp, 2s.

Campaign of Fredericksburg, November—December, 1862. A Study for Officers of Volunteers. With 5 Maps and Plans. Crown 8vo, 5s.

CLERY, *C., Lieut.-Col.*—**Minor Tactics.** With 26 Maps and Plans. Seventh Edition, Revised. Crown 8vo, 9s.

COLVILE, *Lieut. Col. C. F.*—**Military Tribunals.** Sewed, 2s. 6d.

CRAUFURD, *Capt. H. J.*—**Suggestions for the Military Training of a Company of Infantry.** Crown 8vo, 1s. 6d.

HAMILTON, *Capt. Ian, A.D.C.*—**The Fighting of the Future.** 1s.

HARRISON, *Col. R.*—**The Officer's Memorandum Book for Peace and War.** Fourth Edition, Revised throughout. Oblong 32mo, red basil, with pencil, 3s. 6d.

Notes on Cavalry Tactics, Organisation, etc. By a Cavalry Officer. With Diagrams. Demy 8vo, 12s.

PARR, *Capt. H. Hallam, C.M.G.*—**The Dress, Horses, and Equipment of Infantry and Staff Officers.** Crown 8vo, 1s.

SCHAW, *Col. H.*—**The Defence and Attack of Positions and Localities.** Third Edition, Revised and Corrected. Crown 8vo, 3s. 6d.

STONE, *Capt. F. Gleadowe, R.A.*—**Tactical Studies from the Franco-German War of 1870-71.** With 22 Lithographic Sketches and Maps. Demy 8vo, 30s.

WILKINSON, *H. Spenser, Capt. 20th Lancashire R.V.*—**Citizen Soldiers.** Essays towards the Improvement of the Volunteer Force. Crown 8vo, 2s. 6d.

POETRY.

ABBAY, R.—The Castle of Knaresborough. A Tale in Verse. Crown 8vo, 6*s.*

ADAM OF ST. VICTOR.—The Liturgical Poetry of Adam of St. Victor. From the text of GAUTIER. With Translations into English in the Original Metres, and Short Explanatory Notes, by DIGBY S. WRANGHAM, M.A. 3 vols. Crown 8vo, printed on hand-made paper, boards, 21*s.*

AITCHISON, James.—The Chronicle of Mites. A Satire. Small crown 8vo. 5*s.*

ALEXANDER, William, D.D., Bishop of Derry.—St. Augustine's Holiday, and other Poems. Crown 8vo, 6*s.*

AUCHMUTY, A. C.—Poems of English Heroism: From Brunanburh to Lucknow; from Athelstan to Albert. Small crown 8vo, 1*s.* 6*d.*

BARNES, William.—Poems of Rural Life, in the Dorset Dialect. New Edition, complete in one vol. Crown 8vo, 8*s.* 6*d.*

BAYNES, Rev. Canon H. R.—Home Songs for Quiet Hours. Fourth and Cheaper Edition. Fcap. 8vo, cloth, 2*s.* 6*d.*

BEVINGTON, L. S.—Key Notes. Small crown 8vo, 5*s.*

BLUNT, Wilfrid Scawen.—The Wind and the Whirlwind. Demy 8vo, 1*s.* 6*d.*

The Love Sonnets of Proteus. Fifth Edition, 18mo. Cloth extra, gilt top, 5*s.*

BOWEN, H. C., M.A.—Simple English Poems. English Literature for Junior Classes. In Four Parts. Parts I., II., and III., 6*d.* each, and Part IV., 1*s.* Complete, 3*s.*

BRYANT, W. C.—Poems. Cheap Edition, with Frontispiece. Small crown 8vo, 3*s.* 6*d.*

Calderon's Dramas: the Wonder-Working Magician—Life is a Dream—the Purgatory of St. Patrick. Translated by DENIS FLORENCE MACCARTHY. Post 8vo, 10*s.*

Camoens' Lusiads.—Portuguese Text, with Translation by J. J. AUBERTIN. Second Edition. 2 vols. Crown 8vo, 12*s.*

CAMPBELL, Lewis.—Sophocles. The Seven Plays in English Verse. Crown 8vo, 7*s.* 6*d.*

CERVANTES.—Journey to Parnassus. Spanish Text, with Translation into English Tercets, Preface, and Illustrative Notes, by JAMES Y. GIBSON. Crown 8vo, 12*s.*

CERVANTES—continued.

 Numantia: a Tragedy. Translated from the Spanish, with Introduction and Notes, by JAMES Y. GIBSON. Crown 8vo, printed on hand-made paper, 5s.

Chronicles of Christopher Columbus. A Poem in 12 Cantos. By M. D. C. Crown 8vo, 7s. 6d.

Cid Ballads, and other Poems.—Translated from Spanish and German by J. Y. GIBSON. 2 vols. Crown 8vo, 12s.

COXHEAD, Ethel.—**Birds and Babies.** With 33 Illustrations. Imp. 16mo, gilt, 2s. 6d.

Dante's Divina Commedia. Translated in the *Terza Rima* of Original, by F. K. H. HASELFOOT. Demy 8vo, 16s.

DE BERANGER.—**A Selection from his Songs.** In English Verse. By WILLIAM TOYNBEE. Small crown 8vo, 2s. 6d.

DENNIS, J.—**English Sonnets.** Collected and Arranged by. Small crown 8vo, 2s. 6d.

DE VERE, Aubrey.—**Poetical Works.**
 I. THE SEARCH AFTER PROSERPINE, etc. 6s.
 II. THE LEGENDS OF ST. PATRICK, etc. 6s.
 III. ALEXANDER THE GREAT, etc. 6s.

 The Foray of Queen Meave, and other Legends of Ireland's Heroic Age. Small crown 8vo, 5s.

 Legends of the Saxon Saints. Small crown 8vo, 6s.

 Legends and Records of the Church and the Empire. Small crown 8vo, 6s.

DILLON, Arthur.—**Gods and Men.** Fcap. 4to, 7s. 6d.

DOBSON, Austin.—**Old World Idylls and other Verses.** Seventh Edition. Elzevir 8vo, gilt top, 6s.

 At the Sign of the Lyre. Fifth Edition. Elzevir 8vo, gilt top, 6s.

DOWDEN, Edward, LL.D.—**Shakspere's Sonnets.** With Introduction and Notes. Large post 8vo, 7s. 6d.

DUTT, Toru.—**A Sheaf Gleaned in French Fields.** New Edition. Demy 8vo, 10s. 6d.

 Ancient Ballads and Legends of Hindustan. With an Introductory Memoir by EDMUND GOSSE. Second Edition, 18mo. Cloth extra, gilt top, 5s.

EDWARDS, Miss Betham.—**Poems.** Small crown 8vo, 3s. 6d.

ELLIOTT, Ebenezer, The Corn Law Rhymer.—**Poems.** Edited by his son, the Rev. EDWIN ELLIOTT, of St. John's, Antigua. 2 vols. Crown 8vo, 18s.

English Verse. Edited by W. J. LINTON and R. H. STODDARD. 5 vols. Crown 8vo, cloth, 5s. each.
- I. CHAUCER TO BURNS.
- II. TRANSLATIONS.
- III. LYRICS OF THE NINETEENTH CENTURY.
- IV. DRAMATIC SCENES AND CHARACTERS.
- V. BALLADS AND ROMANCES.

FOSKETT, Edward.—Poems. Crown 8vo, 6s.

GOODCHILD, John A.—**Somnia Medici.** Three series. Small crown 8vo, 5s. each.

GOSSE, Edmund.—**New Poems.** Crown 8vo, 7s. 6d.

    Firdausi in Exile, and other Poems. Second Edition. Elzevir 8vo, gilt top, 6s.

GURNEY, Rev. Alfred.—**The Vision of the Eucharist**, and other Poems. Crown 8vo, 5s.

    A Christmas Faggot. Small crown 8vo, 5s.

HARRISON, Clifford.—**In Hours of Leisure.** Crown 8vo, 5s.

HEYWOOD, J. C.—**Herodias**, a Dramatic Poem. New Edition, Revised. Small crown 8vo, 5s.

    Antonius. A Dramatic Poem. New Edition, Revised. Small crown 8vo, 5s.

    Salome. A Dramatic Poem. Small crown 8vo, 5s.

HICKEY, E. H.—**A Sculptor, and other Poems.** Small crown 8vo, 5s.

HOLE, W. G.—**Procris**, and other Poems. Fcap. 8vo, 3s. 6d.

KEATS, John.—**Poetical Works.** Edited by W. T. ARNOLD. Large crown 8vo, choicely printed on hand-made paper, with Portrait in *eau-forte*. Parchment or cloth, 12s.; vellum, 15s.

KING, Edward. **A Venetian Lover.** Small 4to, 6s.

KING, Mrs. Hamilton.—**The Disciples.** Ninth Edition, and Notes. Small crown 8vo, 5s.

    A Book of Dreams. Second Edition. Crown 8vo, 3s. 6d.

LAFFAN, Mrs. R. S. De Courcy.—**A Song of Jubilee, and other Poems.** With Frontispiece. Small crown 8vo, 3s. 6d.

LANG, A.—**XXXII. Ballades in Blue China.** Elzevir 8vo, 5s.

    Rhymes à la Mode. With Frontispiece by E. A. Abbey. Second Edition. Elzevir 8vo, cloth extra, gilt top, 5s.

LANGFORD, J. A., LL.D.—**On Sea and Shore.** Small crown 8vo, 5s.

LASCELLES, John.—**Golden Fetters**, and other Poems. Small crown 8vo, 3s. 6d.

LAWSON, Right Hon. Mr. Justice.—**Hymni Usitati Latine Redditi**: with other Verses. Small 8vo, parchment, 5s.

Living English Poets MDCCCLXXXII. With Frontispiece by Walter Crane. Second Edition. Large crown 8vo. Printed on hand-made paper. Parchment or cloth, 12s.; vellum, 15s.

LOCKER, F.—**London Lyrics.** Tenth Edition. With Portrait, Elzevir 8vo. Cloth extra, gilt top, 5s.

Love in Idleness. A Volume of Poems. With an Etching by W. B. Scott. Small crown 8vo, 5s.

LUMSDEN, Lieut.-Col. H. W.—**Beowulf**: an Old English Poem. Translated into Modern Rhymes. Second and Revised Edition. Small crown 8vo, 5s.

LYSAGHT, Sidney Royse.—**A Modern Ideal.** A Dramatic Poem. Small crown 8vo, 5s.

MAGNUSSON, Eirikr, M.A., and PALMER, E. H., M.A.—**Johan Ludvig Runeberg's Lyrical Songs, Idylls, and Epigrams.** Fcap. 8vo, 5s.

MEREDITH, Owen [The Earl of Lytton].—**Lucile.** New Edition. With 32 Illustrations. 16mo, 3s. 6d. Cloth extra, gilt edges, 4s. 6d.

MORRIS, Lewis.—**Poetical Works of.** New and Cheaper Editions, with Portrait. Complete in 3 vols., 5s. each.
Vol. I. contains "Songs of Two Worlds." Twelfth Edition.
Vol. II. contains "The Epic of Hades." Twenty-first Edition.
Vol. III. contains "Gwen" and "The Ode of Life." Seventh Edition.
Vol. IV. contains "Songs Unsung" and "Gycia." Fifth Edition.

Songs of Britain. Third Edition. Fcap. 8vo, 5s.

The Epic of Hades. With 16 Autotype Illustrations, after the Drawings of the late George R. Chapman. 4to, cloth extra, gilt leaves, 21s.

The Epic of Hades. Presentation Edition. 4to, cloth extra, gilt leaves, 10s. 6d.

The Lewis Morris Birthday Book. Edited by S. S. Copeman, with Frontispiece after a Design by the late George R. Chapman. 32mo, cloth extra, gilt edges, 2s.; cloth limp, 1s. 6d.

MORSHEAD, E. D. A.—**The House of Atreus.** Being the Agamemnon, Libation-Bearers, and Furies of Æschylus. Translated into English Verse. Crown 8vo, 7s.

The Suppliant Maidens of Æschylus. Crown 8vo, 3s. 6d.

MOZLEY, J. Rickards.—**The Romance of Dennell.** A Poem in Five Cantos. Crown 8vo, 7s. 6d.

MULHOLLAND, Rosa.—**Vagrant Verses.** Small crown 8vo, 5s.

NADEN, Constance C. W.—**A Modern Apostle, and other Poems.** Small crown 8vo, 5s.

NOEL, The Hon. Roden.—**A Little Child's Monument.** Third Edition. Small crown 8vo, 3s. 6d.

The House of Ravensburg. New Edition. Small crown 8vo, 6s.

The Red Flag, and other Poems. New Edition. Small crown 8vo, 6s.

Songs of the Heights and Deeps. Crown 8vo, 6s.

O'BRIEN, Charlotte Grace.—**Lyrics.** Small crown 8vo, 3s. 6d.

O'HAGAN, John.—**The Song of Roland.** Translated into English Verse. New and Cheaper Edition. Crown 8vo, 5s.

PFEIFFER, Emily.—**The Rhyme of the Lady of the Rock, and How it Grew.** Second Edition. Small crown 8vo, 3s. 6d.

Gerard's Monument, and other Poems. Second Edition. Crown 8vo, 6s.

Under the Aspens: Lyrical and Dramatic. With Portrait. Crown 8vo, 6s.

PIATT, J. J.—**Idyls and Lyrics of the Ohio Valley.** Crown 8vo, 5s.

PREVOST, Francis.—**Melilot.** 3s. 6d.

Fires of Green Wood. Small crown 8vo, 3s. 6d.

Rare Poems of the 16th and 17th Centuries. Edited by W. J. LINTON. Crown 8vo, 5s.

RHOADES, James.—**The Georgics of Virgil.** Translated into English Verse. Small crown 8vo, 5s.

Poems. Small crown 8vo, 4s. 6d.

Dux Redux. A Forest Tangle. Small crown 8vo, 3s. 6d.

ROBINSON, A. Mary F.—**A Handful of Honeysuckle.** Fcap. 8vo, 3s. 6d.

The Crowned Hippolytus. Translated from Euripides. With New Poems. Small crown 8vo, 5s.

SCHILLER, Friedrich.—**Wallenstein.** A Drama. Done in English Verse, by J. A. W. HUNTER, M.A. Crown 8vo, 7s. 6d.

SCHWARTZ, J. M. W.—**Nivalis.** A Tragedy in Five Acts. Small crown 8vo, 5s.

SCOTT, E. J. L.—**The Eclogues of Virgil.**—Translated into English Verse. Small crown 8vo, 3s. 6d.

SHERBROOKE, Viscount.—**Poems of a Life.** Second Edition. Small crown 8vo, 2s. 6d.

SINCLAIR, Julian.—**Nakiketas, and other Poems.** Small crown 8vo, 2s. 6d.

SMITH, J. W. Gilbart.—**The Loves of Vandyck.** A Tale of Genoa. Small crown 8vo, 2s. 6d.

    The Log o' the "Norseman." Small crown 8vo, 5s.

    Serbelloni. Small crown 8vo, 5s.

Sophocles: The Seven Plays in English Verse. Translated by LEWIS CAMPBELL. Crown 8vo, 7s. 6d.

STEWART, Phillips.—**Poems.** Small crown 8vo, 2s. 6d.

SYMONDS, John Addington.—**Vagabunduli Libellus.** Crown 8vo, 6s.

Tasso's Jerusalem Delivered. Translated by Sir JOHN KINGSTON JAMES, Bart. Two Volumes. Printed on hand-made paper, parchment, bevelled boards. Large crown 8vo, 21s.

TAYLOR, Sir H.—**Works.** Complete in Five Volumes. Crown 8vo, 30s.

    Philip Van Artevelde. Fcap. 8vo, 3s. 6d.

    The Virgin Widow, etc. Fcap. 8vo, 3s. 6d.

    The Statesman. Fcap. 8vo, 3s. 6d.

TODHUNTER, Dr. J.—**Laurella, and other Poems.** Crown 8vo, 6s. 6d.

    Forest Songs. Small crown 8vo, 3s. 6d.

    The True Tragedy of Rienzi: a Drama. 3s. 6d.

    Alcestis: a Dramatic Poem. Extra fcap. 8vo, 5s.

    Helena in Troas. Small crown 8vo, 2s. 6d.

TOMKINS, Zitella E.—**Sister Lucetta, and other Poems.** Small crown 8vo, 3s. 6d.

TYNAN, Katherine.—**Louise de la Vallière, and other Poems.** Small crown 8vo, 3s. 6d.

    Shamrocks. Small crown 8vo, 5s.

Unspoken Thoughts. Small crown 8vo, 3s. 6d.

Victorian Hymns: English Sacred Songs of Fifty Years. Dedicated to the Queen. Large post 8vo, 10s. 6d.

WEBSTER, Augusta.—**In a Day: a Drama.** Small crown 8vo, 2s. 6d.

    Disguises: a Drama. Small crown 8vo, 5s.

WILLIAMS, James.—**A Lawyer's Leisure.** Small crown 8vo, 3s. 6d.

WOOD, *Edmund.*—Poems. Small crown 8vo, 3*s.* 6*d.*

Wordsworth Birthday Book, The. Edited by ADELAIDE and VIOLET WORDSWORTH. 32mo, limp cloth, 1*s.* 6*d.* ; cloth extra, 2*s.*

YOUNGS, *Ella Sharpe.*—Paphus, and other Poems. Small crown 8vo, 3*s.* 6*d.*

    A Heart's Life, Sarpedon, and other Poems. Small crown 8vo, 5*s.* 6*d.*

    The Apotheosis of Antinous, and other Poems. With Portrait. Small crown 8vo, 10*s.* 6*d.*

NOVELS AND TALES.

"All But:" a Chronicle of Laxenford Life. By PEN OLIVER, F.R.C.S. With 20 Illustrations. Second Edition. Crown 8vo, 6*s.*

BANKS, *Mrs. G. L.*—God's Providence House. New Edition. Crown 8vo, 3*s.* 6*d.*

CHICHELE, *Mary.*—Doing and Undoing. A Story. Crown 8vo, 4*s.* 6*d.*

Danish Parsonage. By an Angler. Crown 8vo, 6*s.*

GRAY, *Maxwell.*—The Silence of Dean Maitland. Fifth Edition. With Frontispiece. Crown 8vo, 6*s.*

HUNTER, *Hay.*—The Crime of Christmas Day. A Tale of the Latin Quarter. By the Author of "My Ducats and my Daughter." 1*s.*

HUNTER, *Hay, and* WHYTE, *Walter.*—My Ducats and My Daughter. New and Cheaper Edition. With Frontispiece. Crown 8vo, 6*s.*

INGELOW, *Jean.*—Off the Skelligs: a Novel. With Frontispiece. Second Edition. Crown 8vo, 6*s.*

JENKINS, *Edward.*—A Secret of Two Lives. Crown 8vo, 2*s.* 6*d.*

KIELLAND, *Alexander L.*—Garman and Worse. A Norwegian Novel. Authorized Translation, by W. W. Kettlewell. Crown 8vo, 6*s.*

LANG, *Andrew.*—In the Wrong Paradise, and other Stories. Second Edition. Crown 8vo, 6*s.*

MACDONALD, *G.*—Donal Grant. A Novel. Second Edition. With Frontispiece. Crown 8vo, 6*s.*

    Home Again. With Frontispiece. Crown 8vo, 6*s.*

    Castle Warlock. A Novel. Second Edition. With Frontispiece. Crown 8vo, 6*s.*

MACDONALD, G.—*continued*.

 Malcolm. With Portrait of the Author engraved on Steel. Eighth Edition. Crown 8vo, 6s.

 The Marquis of Lossie. Seventh Edition. With Frontispiece. Crown 8vo, 6s.

 St. George and St. Michael. Fifth Edition. With Frontispiece. Crown 8vo, 6s.

 What's Mine's Mine. Second Edition. With Frontispiece. Crown 8vo, 6s.

 Annals of a Quiet Neighbourhood. Sixth Edition. With Frontispiece. Crown 8vo, 6s.

 The Seaboard Parish: a Sequel to "Annals of a Quiet Neighbourhood." Fourth Edition. With Frontispiece. Crown 8vo, 6s.

 Wilfred Cumbermede. An Autobiographical Story. Fourth Edition. With Frontispiece. Crown 8vo, 6s.

 Thomas Wingfold, Curate. Fourth Edition. With Frontispiece. Crown 8vo, 6s.

 Paul Faber, Surgeon. Fourth Edition. With Frontispiece. Crown 8vo, 6s.

MALET, *Lucas*.—**Colonel Enderby's Wife.** A Novel. New and Cheaper Edition. With Frontispiece. Crown 8vo, 6s.

MULHOLLAND, *Rosa*.—**Marcella Grace.** An Irish Novel. Crown 8vo, 6s.

PALGRAVE, *W. Gifford*.—**Hermann Agha**; an Eastern Narrative. Third Edition. Crown 8vo, 6s.

SHAW, *Flora L*.—**Castle Blair**; a Story of Youthful Days. New and Cheaper Edition. Crown 8vo, 3s. 6d.

STRETTON, *Hesba*.—**Through a Needle's Eye:** a Story. New and Cheaper Edition, with Frontispiece. Crown 8vo, 6s.

TAYLOR, *Col. Meadows, C.S.I., M.R.I.A.*—**Seeta**; a Novel. With Frontispiece. Crown 8vo, 6s.

 Tippoo Sultaun: a Tale of the Mysore War. With Frontispiece. Crown 8vo, 6s.

 Ralph Darnell. With Frontispiece. Crown 8vo, 6s.

 A Noble Queen. With Frontispiece. Crown 8vo, 6s.

 The Confessions of a Thug. With Frontispiece. Crown 8vo, 6s.

 Tara; a Mahratta Tale. With Frontispiece. Crown 8vo, 6s.

Within Sound of the Sea. With Frontispiece. Crown 8vo, 6s.

BOOKS FOR THE YOUNG.

Brave Men's Footsteps. A Book of Example and Anecdote for Young People. By the Editor of "Men who have Risen." With 4 Illustrations by C. Doyle. Ninth Edition. Crown 8vo, 3s. 6d.

COXHEAD, *Ethel.*—Birds and Babies. With 33 Illustrations. Second Edition. Imp. 16mo, cloth-gilt, 2s. 6d.

DAVIES, *G. Christopher.*—Rambles and Adventures of our School Field Club. With 4 Illustrations. New and Cheaper Edition. Crown 8vo, 3s. 6d.

EDMONDS, *Herbert.*—Well Spent Lives: a Series of Modern Biographies. New and Cheaper Edition. Crown 8vo, 3s. 6d.

EVANS, *Mark.*—The Story of our Father's Love, told to Children. Sixth and Cheaper Edition of Theology for Children. With 4 Illustrations. Fcap. 8vo, 1s. 6d.

MAC KENNA, *S. J.*—Plucky Fellows. A Book for Boys. With 6 Illustrations. Fifth Edition. Crown 8vo, 3s. 6d.

MALET, *Lucas.*—Little Peter. A Christmas Morality for Children of any Age. With numerous Illustrations. 5s.

REANEY, *Mrs. G. S.*—Waking and Working; or, From Girlhood to Womanhood. New and Cheaper Edition. With a Frontispiece. Crown 8vo, 3s. 6d.

    Blessing and Blessed: a Sketch of Girl Life. New and Cheaper Edition. Crown 8vo, 3s. 6d.

    Rose Gurney's Discovery. A Story for Girls. Dedicated to their Mothers. Crown 8vo, 3s. 6d.

    English Girls: Their Place and Power. With Preface by the Rev. R. W. Dale. Fifth Edition. Fcap. 8vo, 2s. 6d.

    Just Anyone, and other Stories. Three Illustrations. Royal 16mo, 1s. 6d.

    Sunbeam Willie, and other Stories. Three Illustrations. Royal 16mo, 1s. 6d.

    Sunshine Jenny, and other Stories. Three Illustrations. Royal 16mo, 1s. 6d.

STORR, *Francis, and* TURNER, *Hawes.*—Canterbury Chimes; or, Chaucer Tales re-told to Children. With 6 Illustrations from the Ellesmere Manuscript. Third Edition. Fcap. 8vo, 3s. 6d.

STRETTON, *Hesba.*—David Lloyd's Last Will. With 4 Illustrations. New Edition. Royal 16mo, 2s. 6d.

WHITAKER, *Florence.*—Christy's Inheritance. A London Story. Illustrated. Royal 16mo, 1s. 6d.

PRINTED BY WILLIAM CLOWES AND SONS, LIMITED,
LONDON AND BECCLES.

MESSRS.
KEGAN PAUL, TRENCH & CO.'S
EDITIONS OF
SHAKSPERE'S WORKS.

THE PARCHMENT LIBRARY EDITION.

THE AVON EDITION.

The Text of these Editions is mainly that of Delius. Wherever a variant reading is adopted, some good and recognized Shaksperian Critic has been followed. In no case is a new rendering of the text proposed; nor has it been thought necessary to distract the reader's attention by notes or comments.

1, PATERNOSTER SQUARE.   [P. T. O.

SHAKSPERE'S WORKS.

THE AVON EDITION.

Printed on thin opaque paper, and forming 12 handy volumes, cloth, 18*s.*, or bound in 6 volumes, 15*s.*

The set of 12 volumes may also be had in a cloth box, price 21*s.*, or bound in Roan, Persian, Crushed Persian Levant, Calf, or Morocco, and enclosed in an attractive leather box at prices from 31*s.* 6*d.* upwards.

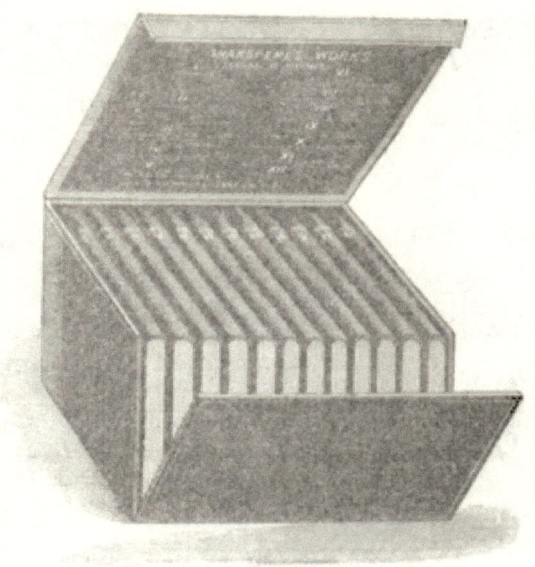

SOME PRESS NOTICES.

"This edition will be useful to those who want a good text, well and clearly printed, in convenient little volumes that will slip easily into an overcoat pocket or a travelling-bag."—*St. James's Gazette.*

"We know no prettier edition of Shakspere for the price."—*Academy.*

"It is refreshing to meet with an edition of Shakspere of convenient size and low price, without either notes or introductions of any sort to distract the attention of the reader."—*Saturday Review.*

"It is exquisite. Each volume is handy, is beautifully printed, and in every way lends itself to the taste of the cultivated student of Shakspere."—*Scotsman.*

LONDON: KEGAN PAUL, TRENCH & CO., 1, PATERNOSTER SQUARE.

www.ingramcontent.com/pod-product-compliance
Lightning Source LLC
Chambersburg PA
CBHW021821230426
43669CB00008B/829